M000303967

THE
ECCLESIASTICAL
HISTORY
OF
EVAGRIUS

A HISTORY OF THE CHURCH
FROM AD 431 TO AD 594

Translated with an introduction by
Edward Walford

Evolution Publishing
Merchantville NJ
2008

Originally Published by
Samuel Bagster and Sons, London
1846

This edition ©2008 by Evolution Publishing
Merchantville, New Jersey.

Printed in the United States of America

ISBN 978-1-889758-88-6

Library of Congress Cataloging-in-Publication Data

Evagrius, Scholasticus, b. 536?
  The ecclesiastical history of Evagrius : a history of the church
from ad 431 to ad 594 / translated with an introduction by Edward
Walford.
      p. cm. -- (Christian Roman empire series ; v. 5)
  Originally published: London : Samuel Bagster and Son, 1846.
  Includes index.
  ISBN 978-1-889758-88-6
  1. Church history--Primitive and early church, ca. 30-600.
I. Title.
  BR160.E7E5 2008
  270.2--dc22
                                    2007049435

TABLE OF CONTENTS
TO THE 2008 EDITION

THE ECCLESIASTICAL HISTORY OF EVAGRIUS

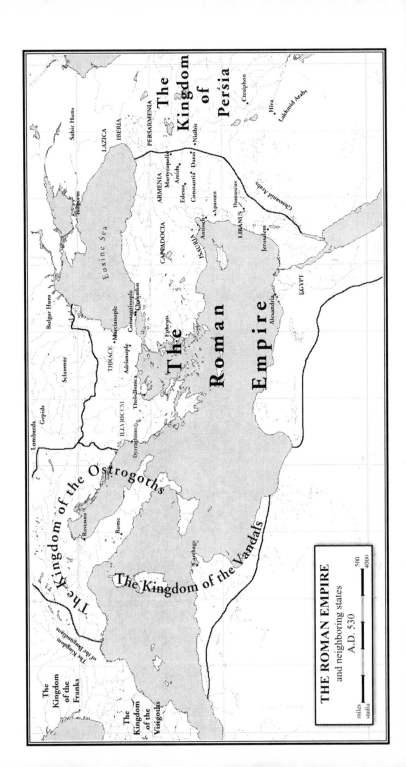

THE ROMAN EMPIRE
and neighboring states
A.D. 530

PREFACE TO THE 2008 EDITION

The *Ecclesiastical History* of Evagrius Scholasticus is an intriguing though under-appreciated work of the late 6th century AD which deserves wider consideration among modern audiences. In his prologue, Evagrius styles himself as a continuator of the great Church historians Eusebius, Socrates, Sozomen, and Theodoret. Yet, particularly as he approaches his own time, it becomes clear that Evagrius has cast a wider net than his predecessors. While never straying from his purpose as an elucidator of God's Providence and a defender of Chalcedonian orthodoxy, Evagrius records a great deal of information from both religious and temporal history—much of it personal—that would have otherwise been lost.

The first section of his work deals almost exclusively with ecclesiastical issues, such as the heresy and death of Nestorius, the Council of Ephesus (AD 431), the second Council of Ephesus (the so-called "Robber Council" of AD 449), the Council of Chalcedon (AD 451), the circular and counter-circular of Basiliscus (AD 475-6), and the Henoticon of the emperor Zeno (AD 482). For these important moments in Church history, Evagrius is a first-class source—for some of them, such as the Circular and Countercircular of Basiliscus, and the Henoticon of Zeno, he is the sole source in the original Greek.[1] In composing his history, Evagrius also drew upon other valuable tracts that are now either severely truncated or lost all together, including the works of Eustathius, Zachariah Scholasticus, and John of Epiphania.[2]

But what makes Evagrius most interesting is his inclusion of testimony specific to himself and his home region. Born in the mid-530s, Evagrius witnessed the devastation of Roman Syria by the Persians and experienced first-hand the great plague which swept the Mediterranean world beginning in the 540s. He had first-hand knowledge of the myriad saints and scoundrels who lived in his time, and he witnessed the miracles and catastrophes that occurred with astounding regularity. His testimony is occasionally credulous but at the same time generally right-headed and trustworthy.

The original text of this translation of Evagrius was published anonymously as part of the series entitled *Greek Ecclesiastical Historians of the First Six Centuries of the Christian Era* in 1846. I have attributed it to Edward Walford based on the research of Roger Pearse, creator of the incredibly useful www.tertullian.org website.[3] Mr. Pearse discovered Walford's authorship by conducting an online search of the holdings of the Bodleian Library, Oxford, UK. Having performed the same search myself, I can confirm his findings and have no reason to assume the Bodleian has erred here.

This reprint of Walford's translation of Evagrius is intended for students and the general reader. Aside from a shift in spelling style from British to American, a general updating of punctuation, and the adding of paragraph markers, Walford's prose is retained without change. This edition also includes a few additional notes at the end of each chapter by the current editor, but is otherwise light on commentary. For the specialist, Michael Whitby's 2000 translation of Evagrius, complete with extraordinarily thorough commentary, is an excellent resource. Also eminently worthy of consultation by the specialist is Pauline Allen's scholarly study, *Evagrius Scholasticus The Church Historian.*

—*Anthony P. Schiavo, Jr.*
Merchantville, NJ
November, 2007

NOTES

1. Allen, p. 6.
2. Allen, pp. 7–10.
3. See http://www.tertullian.org/fathers/evagrius_0_intro2.htm

2008 EDITION BIBLIOGRAPHY AND FURTHER READING

Adams, Francis. 1834. *The Medical Works of Paulus Ægineta, the Greek Physician.* Welsh, Treuttel, Würtz & Co.: London.

Agathias Scholasticus. Joseph D. Frendo (transl.) 1975. *The Histories.* Walter de Gruyter: Berlin/New York.

Allen, Pauline. 1981. *Evagrius Scholasticus: The Church Historian.* Spicilegium Sacrum Lovaniense: Leuven.

Bury, J. B. 1958 [1923]. *History of the Later Roman Empire: From the Death of Theodosius I to the Death of Justinian.* Vols. I and II. Dover Publications: Mineola, NY.

Chestnut, Glenn F. 1986. *The First Christian Histories.* Second Edition. Mercer University Press: Macon, GA.

Dawes, Elizabeth and Norman H. Baynes (transl.) 1977. *Three Byzantine Saints: Contemporary Biographies of St. Daniel the Stylite, St. Theodore of Sykeon, and St. John the Almsgiver.* St. Vladimir's Seminary Press. Crestwood, NY.

Evagrius Scholasticus. Michael Whitby (transl.) 2000, *The Ecclesiastical History of Evagrius Scholasticus.* Liverpool University Press: Liverpool, UK.

Ferguson, Everett et al. (eds.) 1998. *Encyclopedia of Early Christianity.* Garland Publishing: New York.

Herbermann, Charles G., et al. 1913. *The Catholic Encyclopedia: An International Work of Reference on the Constitution, Doctrine, Discipline, and History of the Catholic Church.* The Encyclopedia Press: New York. Electronic edition available online at http://www.newadvent.org/cathen/

John Malalas. Elizabeth Jeffreys, Michael Jeffreys and Roger Scott (transl.) 1986. *The Chronicle of John Malalas: A Translation.* Australian Association for Byzantine Studies: Melbourne, Australia.

John, Bishop of Nikiu. R. H. Charles (transl.) 2007 [1916]. *The Chronicle of John, Bishop of Nikiu:* Translated from Zotenberg's Ethiopic Text. Evolution Publishing: Merchantville, NJ.

Joshua the Stylite. Frank R. Trombley & Joseph W. Watt (transl.) 2001. *The Chronicle of Pseudo-Joshua the Stylite.* Liverpool University Press: Liverpool, UK.

March, Jenny. 1998. *Cassell's Dictionary of Classical Mythology.* Cassell: London.

Procopius. H. B. Dewing (transl.) 1916. *History of the Wars Books I–VIII.* Vols. 1–5. Harvard University Press: Cambridge, MA.

Procopius. H. B. Dewing (transl.) 1916. *Buildings.* Vol. 6. Harvard University Press: Cambridge, MA.

Procopius. G. A. Williamson (transl.) 1966. *The Secret History.* Penguin Books: London.

Socrates Scholasticus. E. Walford (transl.) 1853. *The Ecclesiastical History of Socrates, Surnamed Scholasticus, or the Advocate.* Samuel Bagster: London.

Sozomen. E. Walford (transl.) 1855. *The Ecclesiastical History of Sozomen.* Samuel Bagster: London.

Theodoret. E. Walford (transl.) 1843. *The Ecclesiastical History of Theodoret.* Samuel Bagster: London.

Theophylact Simocatta. Michael Whitby and Mary Whitby (transl.) 1986. *The History of Theophylact Simocatta.* Clarendon Press: Oxford.

Wilson, Ian 1998. *The Blood and the Shroud.* The Free Press: New York.

Zachariah of Mitylene. F. J. Hamilton & E. W. Brooks (transl.) 1899. *The Syriac Chronicle Known as that of Zachariah of Mitylene.* Methuen & Co.: London.

Zosimus. R. Ridley (transl.) 1982. *New History.* Australian Association for Byzantine Studies: Melbourne, Australia.

INTRODUCTION
TO THE 1846 EDITION

ACCOUNT OF THE AUTHOR
AND HIS WRITINGS

The very few particulars which are known respecting the author of the following History, are gathered from the history itself. Evagrius was a native of Epiphania on the Orontes, and his birth may be fixed about AD 536. He was by profession a Scholasticus, or advocate, and by this title he is commonly distinguished from other persons of the same name. The earliest circumstance which the historian mentions respecting himself, is his visit when a child, in company with his parents, to Apamea, to witness the solemn display of the wood of the cross, amidst the consternation caused by the sack of Antioch by Chosroes (Book IV. chap. xxvi). The history, in many places, shows a minute familiarity with the localities of Antioch: and the prominent interest which the writer variously manifests in that city and its fortunes, can only be accounted for by supposing that it was his ordinary residence, and the principal scene of his professional practice. In his description of the great pestilence which continued its ravages throughout the empire for more than fifty years, he mentions that he himself was attacked by the disease in his childhood, and that subsequently he lost by it his first wife, besides several relatives and members of his household, and among them in particular a daughter with her child (Book IV. chap. xxix).

Evagrius accompanied Gregory, patriarch of Antioch, as his professional adviser, when he appeared before a synod at Constantinople to clear himself from a charge of incest (Book

VI. chap. vii). On his return to Antioch after the acquittal of the patriarch, he married a young wife: and a proof of the important position which he occupied, is incidentally afforded by the circumstance that his nuptials were made an occasion for a public festival (Book VI. chap. viii). Some of his memorials, drawn up in the service of the patriarch, obtained for him from the emperor Tiberius the honorary rank of Exquæstor; and a composition on occasion of the birth of an heir to the emperor Maurice was rewarded with the higher dignity of Expræfect (Book VI. chap. xxiv). With the mention of these last circumstances the history closes.

The only extant work of Evagrius is the "Ecclesiastical History," commencing with the rise of the Nestorian controversy, and ending with the twelfth year of the reign of Maurice. He professes, at the outset, an intention of including in his narrative matters other than ecclesiastical; and this he has done so far as to give a secular appearance to some parts of it. As might be expected from an author of that period, his style is frequently affected and redundant. The modern reader will, however, be principally struck by the credulity manifested in his cordial detail of prodigies and miracles. But on this point it must be remembered, that the bent of the age was strongly in favor of the marvelous: and this frame of the public mind was a soil which would both spontaneously produce an abundant crop of wonders, in a fond distortion and exaggeration of ordinary occurrences, and also would not fail to be cultivated by the hand of imposture. This feature of the historian's character ought therefore in no way to affect his reputation for honesty, or his claim to general credence. It is only a proof that he was not one of the few whose intellectual course is independent of the habits of their age. There is no reason for confounding him with those in whom a heated mind has at length admitted the idea, that the maintenance of what is believed to be a good cause may be rightfully aided by attestations knowingly bestowed upon falsehoods. Upon the whole, the preservation of his work must be a matter of satisfaction to the studious in history, whether ecclesiastical or civil. It was used by Nicephorus Callisti in the composition of his own History, and has received a favorable notice in the Myriobiblion of the patriarch Photius.

Evagrius also published a collection of his memorials and miscellaneous compositions, which may now be regarded as lost (Book VI. chap. xxiv). He also intimates an intention (Book V. chap. xx) of composing a distinct work, embracing an account of the operations of Maurice against the Persians; but there is no reason for supposing that this design was ever executed.

TABLE OF CONTENTS

THE HISTORY—BOOK I

THE HISTORY—BOOK II

THE HISTORY—BOOK III

THE HISTORY—BOOK IV

THE HISTORY—BOOK V

THE HISTORY—BOOK VI

THE ECCLESIASTICAL HISTORY OF EVAGRIUS

THE FIRST BOOK

PREFACE. DESIGN OF THE WORK.

Eusebius Pamphili—an especially able writer, to the extent, in particular, of inducing his readers to embrace our religion, though failing to perfect them in the faith—and Sozomen, Theodoret, and Socrates have produced a most excellent record of the advent of our compassionate God, and His ascension into heaven, and of all that has been achieved in the endurance of the divine Apostles, as well as of the other martyrs; and, further, of whatever events have occurred among us, whether more or less worthy of mention, down to a certain period of the reign of Theodosius.

But since events subsequent, and scarcely inferior to these, have not hitherto been made the subject of continuous narrative, I have resolved, though but ill-qualified for such a task, to undertake the labor which the subject demands, and to embody them in a history; surely trusting in Him who enlightened fishermen, and endued a brute tongue with articulate utterance, for ability to raise up transactions already entombed in oblivion, to reanimate them by language, and immortalize them by memory: my object being, that my readers may learn the nature of each of these events, up to our time; the period place, and manner of its occurrence, as well as those who were its objects and authors; and that no circumstance worthy of recollection, may be lost under the veil of listless indifference or its neighbor, forgetfulness. I shall then begin, led onwards by the divine impulse, from the point where the above-mentioned writers closed the history.

CHAPTER I

ARTIFICE BY WHICH THE DEVIL ATTEMPTS TO SUBVERT THE PURITY OF THE FAITH.

Scarce had the impiety of Julian been flooded over by the blood of the martyrs, and the frenzy of Arius been bound fast in the fetters forged at Nicæa, and, moreover, Eunomius and Macedonius, by the agency of the Holy Spirit, had been swept as by a blast to the Bosphorus, and wrecked against the sacred city of Constantine; scarce had the holy church cast off her recent defilement, and was being restored to her ancient beauty, robed in a vesture inwrought with gold, and in varied array, and becoming meet for the bridegroom, when the demon enemy of good, unable to lure it, commences against us a new mode of warfare, disdaining idolatry, now laid in the dust, nor deigning to employ, the servile madness of Arius. He fears to assault the faith in open war, embattled by so many holy fathers, and he had been already shorn of nearly all his power in battling against it: but he pursues his purpose with a robber's stealth, by raising certain questions and answers; his new device being turn the course of error towards Judaism, little foreseeing the overthrow that hence would befall the miserable designer. For the faith which formerly was alone arrayed against him, this he now affects: and, no longer exulting in the thought of forcing us to abandon the whole, but of succeeding in corrupting a single term, while he wound himself with many a malignant wile, he devised the change of merely a letter, tending indeed to the same sense, but still with the intention of severing the thought and the tongue, that both

2

might no longer with one accord offer the same confession and glorification to God.

The manner and result of these transactions I will set forth, each at its proper juncture; giving at the same time a place in my narrative to other matters that may occur to me, which, though not belonging to my immediate subject, are worthy of mention, laying up the record of them wherever it shall please our compassionate God.

CHAPTER II

HERESY OF NESTORIUS DISCOVERED AND CONDEMNED.

Since, then, Nestorius, that God-assaulting tongue, that second conclave of Caiaphas, that workshop of blasphemy, in whose case Christ is again made a subject of bargain and sale, by having His natures divided and torn asunder—He of whom not a single bone was broken even on the cross, according to Scripture, and whose seamless vest suffered no rending at the hands of God-slaying men—since, then, he thrust aside and rejected the term, Mother of God, which had been already wrought by the Holy Spirit through the instrumentality of many chosen fathers, and substituted a spurious one of his own coining—Mother of Christ; and further filled the Church with innumerable wars, deluging it with kindred blood, I think that I shall be at a loss for a well-judged arrangement of my history, nor miss its end, if, with the aid of Christ, who is God over all, I preface it with the impious blasphemy of Nestorius.

The war of the churches took its rise from the following circumstances. A certain presbyter named Anastasius, a man of corrupt opinions, and a warm admirer of Nestorius and his Jewish sentiments, who also accompanied him when setting out from his country to take possession of his bishopric; at which time Nestorius, having met with Theodore at Mopsuestia, was

3

perverted by his teaching from godly doctrine, as Theodulus writes in an epistle upon this subject—this Anastasius, in discoursing to the Christ-loving people in the church of Constantinople, dared to say, without any reserve, "Let no one style Mary the Mother of God; for Mary was human, and it is impossible for God to be born of a human being."

When the Christ-loving people were disgusted, and with reason regarded his discourse as blasphemous, Nestorius, the real teacher of the blasphemy, so far from restraining him and upholding the true doctrine, on the contrary, imparted to the teaching of Anastasius the impulse it acquired, by urging on the question with more than ordinary pugnacity. And further, by mingling with it notions of his own, and thus vomiting forth the venom of his soul, he endeavored to inculcate opinions still more blasphemous, proceeding so far as thus to avouch, upon his own peril, "I could never be induced to call that God which admitted of being two months old or three months old." These circumstances rest on the distinct authority of Socrates, and former synod at Ephesus.

CHAPTER III

LETTER FROM CYRIL TO NESTORIUS. COUNCIL OF EPHESUS.

When Cyril, the renowned bishop of the church of the Alexandrians, had communicated to Nestorius his reprobation of these transactions, and he in rejoinder paid no regard to what was addressed to him by Cyril and by Celestine, bishop of the elder Rome, but was irreverently pouring forth his own vomit over the whole church, there was just occasion for the convening of the first synod of Ephesus, at the injunction the younger Theodosius, sovereign of the Eastern empire, by the issuing of imperial letters to Cyril and the presidents of the holy churches in every quarter naming, at the same time, as the day of meeting, the sacred Pentecost, on which the life-giving Spirit descended upon us.

Nestorius, on account of the short distance of Ephesus from Constantinople, arrives early; and Cyril too, with his company, came before the appointed day; but John, the president of the church of Antioch, with his associate bishops, was behind the appointed time; not intentionally, as defense has been thought by many to have sufficiently proved, but because he could not muster his associates with sufficient dispatch, who were at a distance of what would be a twelve days' journey to an expeditious traveler from the city formerly named from Antiochus but now the City of God,[1] and in some cases more; and Ephesus was then just thirty days' journey from Antioch. He stoutly defended himself on the ground that the observance of what is called the New Lord's Day by his bishops in their respective sees was an insuperable impediment to his arriving before the stated day.

CHAPTER IV

DEPOSITION OF NESTORIUS.

When fifteen days had elapsed from the prescribed period, the bishops who had assembled for this business considering that the Orientals would not join them at all, or, at least, after a considerable delay, hold a conclave under the presidency of the divine Cyril, occupying the post of AD 431 Celestine who, as has been before mentioned, was bishop of the elder Rome. They accordingly summon Nestorius, with an exhortation that he would defend himself against the allegations.

When, however, notwithstanding a promise given on the preceding day, that he would present himself if there were occasion, he did not appear, though thrice summoned, the assembly proceeded to the investigation of the matter. Memnon, the president of the Ephesian church, recounted the days which had elapsed, fifteen in number: then were read the letters addressed to Nestorius by the divine Cyril and his rejoinders; there being also inserted the sacred epistle of the illustrious Celestine to Nestorius himself. Theodotus, bishop of Ancyra, and Acacius of Melitene, also detailed the blasphemous language to which Nestorius had unreservedly given utterance at Ephesus. With these were combined many statements in which holy fathers had purely set forth the true faith, having side by side with them various blasphemies which the frenzy of the impious Nestorius had vented. When all this had been done, the holy synod declared its judgment precisely in the following terms:

"Since, in addition to the other matters, the most reverend Nestorius has refused to submit to our summons, or yet to admit the most holy and godly bishops who were sent by us, we have of necessity proceeded to the investigation of his impieties: and having convicted him of entertaining and avowing impious sentiment, on the evidence both of his letters and writings which have been read, and also of words uttered by him lately in this metropolitan city, and established by sufficient testimony, at length, compelled by the canons, and in accordance with the epistle of our most holy father and fellow-minister, Celestine, bishop of the church of Rome, we have, with many tears, proceeded to this sad sentence. The Lord Jesus Christ who has been blasphemed by him, has, through the agency of this holy synod, decreed, that the same Nestorius is alien from the episcopal dignity, and from every sacerdotal assembly."

CHAPTER V

DEPOSITION OF CYRIL AND OF JOHN.
THEIR RECONCILIATION.

After the delivery of this most legitimate and just sentence, John, the bishop of Antioch, arrives with his associate priests, five days after the act of deposition; and having convened all his company, he deposes Cyril and Memnon. On account, however, of libels[2] put forth by Cyril and Memnon to the synod which had been assembled in company with themselves (although Socrates, in ignorance, has given a different account), John is summoned to justify the deposition which he had pronounced; and, on his not appearing after a thrice repeated summons, Cyril and Memnon are released from their sentence, and John and his priests are cut off from the holy communion and all sacerdotal authority.

When, however, Theodosius, notwithstanding his refusal at first to sanction the deposition of Nestorius, had subsequently, on being fully informed of his blasphemy, addressed pious letters to Cyril and John, they are reconciled to each other, and ratify the act of deposition.

CHAPTER VI

CYRIL'S EULOGY OF A LETTER FROM JOHN OF ANTIOCH.

On occasion of the arrival of Paul, bishop of Emesa at Alexandria, and his delivery before the church of that discourse which is extant on this subject, Cyril also, after highly commending the epistle of John wrote to him in these words:

"Let the heavens rejoice and the earth be glad, for the middle wall of partition is broken down, exasperation is stilled, and all occasion for dissension utterly removed through the bestowal of peace upon his churches by Christ, the Savior of us all; at the call, too, of our most religious and divinely favored sovereigns, who, in excellent imitation of ancestral piety, preserve in their own souls a well-founded and unshaken maintenance of the true faith, and a singular care for the holy churches that they may acquire an everlasting renown, and render their reign most glorious. On them the Lord of Hosts himself bestows blessings with a bountiful

7

hand, and grants them victory over their adversaries. Victory He does bestow: for never can he lie who says, 'As I live, saith the Lord, those that glorify me, I glorify.'[3] On the arrival, then, of my most pious brother and fellow minister, my lord Paul, at Alexandria, I was filled with delight, and with great reason, at the mediation of such a man, and his voluntary engagement in labors beyond his strength, in order that he might subdue the malice of the devil, close our breaches, and, by the removal of the stumbling-blocks that lay between us, might crown both our churches and yours with unanimity and peace."

And presently he proceeds thus: "That the dissension of the church has been altogether unnecessary and without sufficient ground I am fully convinced, now that my lord the most pious bishop Paul has brought a paper presenting an unexceptionable confession of the faith, and has assured me that it was drawn up by your holiness and the most pious bishops of your country."

And such is the writing thus drawn up, and inserted verbatim, in the epistle; which, with reference to the Mother of God, speaks as follows: "When we read these your sacred words, and were conscious that our own sentiments were correspondent—for there is one Lord, one faith, one baptism—we glorified God, the Preserver of all things, with a feeling of mutual joy, that both your churches and ours maintain a faith in agreement with the divinely inspired Scriptures and the tradition of our holy fathers."

Of these matters any one may be assured, who is disposed to investigate diligently the transactions of those times.

CHAPTER VII

DEATH OF NESTORIUS.

Historians have not detailed either the banishment of Nestorius, his subsequent fortunes, or the manner in which his life was closed, and the retribution with which he was visited for his blasphemy; matters which would have been allowed to slip into oblivion, and have been altogether swallowed up by time, so as not to be current even in hearsay, if I had not met with a book written by himself, which supplied an account of them.

Nestorius, then, himself, the father of the blasphemy, who raised his structure not on the foundation already laid, but built upon the sand one which, in accordance with the Lord's parable, quickly fell to ruin, here, in addition to other matters of his choice, puts forth a defense of his own blasphemy, in reply to those who had charged him with unnecessary innovation and an unseemly demand for the convening of the synod at Ephesus. He asserts that he was driven to assume this position by absolute necessity, on account of the division of the church into two parties, one maintaining that Mary ought to be styled Mother of Man; the other, Mother of God; and he devised the title, Mother of Christ, in order, as he says, that error might not be incurred by adopting either extreme, either a term which too closely united immortal essence with humanity, or one which, while admitting one of the two natures, involved no mention of the other. He also intimates that Theodosius, from feelings of friendship, withheld his ratification of the sentence of deposition; and, afterwards, that, on occasion of the mission of several bishops of both parties from Ephesus to the emperor, and, moreover, at his own request, he was allowed to retire to his own monastery, situated without the gates of the city now called Theopolis. It is not, indeed, expressly named by Nestorius, but is said to be that which is now styled the monastery of Euprepius; which we know to be, in fact, not more than two stadia from that city.

Nestorius, then, himself says, that during a residence there of four years, he received every mark of respect and distinction; and that, by a second edict of Theodosius, he is banished to the place called Oasis. But the pith of the matter he has suppressed. For in his retirement he did not cease from his peculiar blasphemy; so that John, the president of the church of Antioch, was led to report the circumstance, and Nestorius was, in consequence, condemned to perpetual banishment.

He has addressed also a formal discourse to a certain Egyptian, on the subject of his banishment to Oasis, where he treats of these circumstances more fully. But the retribution with which, unable to escape the all-seeing eye, he was visited for blasphemous imaginations, may be gathered from other writings addressed by him to the governor of the Thebaid: in which one may see how that, since he had not yet reached the full measure of his deserts, the vengeance of God visited him, in pursuance, with the most terrible of all calamities, captivity. Being, then, still deserving of greater penalties, he was liberated by the Blemmyes, into whose hands he had fallen and, after Theodosius had decreed his return to his place of exile, wandering from place to place on the verge of the Thebaid, and severely injured by a fall he closed his life in a manner worthy of his deeds whose fate, like that of Arius, was a judicial declaration, what are the appointed wages of blasphemy against Christ: for both committed similar blasphemy against Him; the one by calling Him a creature; the other regarding Him as human.

When Nestorius impugns the integrity of the acts of the council of Ephesus, and refers them to subtle designs and lawless innovation on the part of Cyril, I should be most ready thus to reply: How came it to pass, that he was banished even by Theodosius, notwithstanding his friendly feelings towards him, and was condemned by repeated sentences of extermination, and closed this life under those unhappy circumstances? If Cyril and his associate priests were not guided by heaven in their judgment, how came it to pass that, when both parties were no longer numbered with the living, in which case a heathen sage[4] has observed, "A frank and kindly meed is yielded to departed worth," the one is reprobated as a blasphemer and enemy of God, the other is lauded and proclaimed to the world as the sonorous herald and mighty champion of true doctrine? In order that I may not incur a charge of slander, let me bring Nestorius himself into court as an evidence on these points. Read me then word for word, some passages of thy epistle, addressed to the governor of the Thebaid:

"On account of the matters which have been lately mooted at Ephesus concerning our holy religion, Oasis, further called Ibis has been appointed as the place of my residence by imperial decree."

And presently he proceeds thus: "Inasmuch as the beforementioned place has fallen into the hands of the barbarians, and been reduced to utter desolation by fire and sword, and I, by most unexpected act of compassion, have been liberated by them, with a menacing injunction instantly to fly from the spot, since the Mazices were upon the point of succeeding them in their occupation of it; I have, accordingly, reached the Thebaid, together with the captive survivors whom they had joined me, by an act of pity for which I am unable to account. They, accordingly, have been allowed to disperse themselves to the places whither their individual inclinations led them, and I, proceeding to Panopolis, have showed myself in public, for fear lest anyone, making the circumstance of my seizure an occasion of criminal proceeding, should raise a charge against me, either of escaping from my place of exile, or some other imagined delinquency: for malice never wants occasion for slander.

"Therefore I entreat your highness to take that just view of my seizure which the laws would enjoin, and not sacrifice a prisoner of war to the malice and evil designs of men: lest there should hence arise this melancholy story with all posterity, that it is better to be made captive by barbarians, than to fly for refuge to the protection of the Roman sovereignty."

He then prefers, with solemn adjuration, the following request: "I request you to lay before the emperor the circumstance, that my arrival hither from Oasis arose from my liberation by the barbarians; so that my final disposal, according to God's good pleasure, may now be determined."

The second epistle, from the same to the same, contains as follows: "Whether you are disposed to regard this present letter as a friendly communication from me to your highness, or as an admonition from a father to a son, I beseech you bear with its detail, embracing, indeed, many matters, but as briefly as the case would allow. When Ibis has been devastated by a numerous body of Nomades," and so forth. "Under these circumstances, by what motive or pretext on the part of your highness I know not, I was conducted by barbarous soldiers from Panopolis to Elephantine, a place on the verge of the province of the Thebaid, being dragged thither by the aforesaid military force; and when, sorely shattered, I had accomplished the greater part of the journey, I am encountered by an unwritten order from your valor to return to Panopolis.

"Thus, miserably worn with the casualties of the road, with a body afflicted by disease and age, and a mangled hand and side, I arrived at Panopolis in extreme exhaustion, and further tormented with cruel pains: whence a second written injunction from your valor, speedily overtaking me, transported me to its adjacent territory. While I was supposing that this treatment would now cease, and was awaiting the determination of our glorious sovereigns respecting me, another merciless order was suddenly issued for a fourth deportation."

And presently he proceeds: "I pray you to rest satisfied with what has been done, and with having inflicted so many banishments on one individual. And I call upon you kindly to leave to our glorious sovereigns the inquisitions for which reports laid before them by your highness, and by myself too, by whom it was proper information should be given, would furnish materials. If, however, this should excite your indignation, continue to deal with me as before, according to your pleasure; since no words can prevail over your will."

Thus does this man, who had not learned moderation even by his sufferings, in his writings strike and trample with fist and heel, even reviling both the supreme and provincial governments. I learn from one who wrote an account of his demise, that, when his tongue had been eaten through with worms, he departed to the greater and everlasting judgment which awaited him.

CHAPTER VIII

SUCCESSION OF BISHOPS AT CONSTANTINOPLE.

Next in succession to that malignant spirit Nestorius, Maximianus is invested with the bishopric of the city of the renowned Constantine, in whose time the church of God enjoyed perfect peace: and when he was departed from among men, Proclus holds the helm of the see, who had some time before been ordained bishop of Cyzicus. When he too had gone the way of all mankind, Flavian succeeds to the see.

CHAPTER IX

HERESY OF EUTYCHES.

In his time arose the stir about the impious Eutyches, when a partial synod was assembled in Constantinople, and a written charge was preferred by Eusebius, bishop of Dorylæum, who, while still practicing as a rhetorician, was the first to expose the blasphemy of Nestorius. Since Eutyches, when summoned, did not appear, and afterwards, even on his appearance, was convicted on certain points; for he had said, "I allow that our Lord was produced from two natures before their union, but I confess only one nature after their union;" and he even maintained that our Lord's body was not of the same substance with ourselves—on these grounds he is sentenced to deprivation; but on his presenting a petition to Theodosius, on the plea that the acts, as set forth, had been concocted in the hands of Flavian, the synod of the neighboring region is assembled at Constantinople, and Flavian is tried by it and some of the magistrates; and when the truth of the acts had been confirmed, the second synod at Ephesus is summoned.

CHAPTER X

PROCEEDINGS OF THE SECOND COUNCIL OF EPHESUS.

Of this council, Dioscorus, the successor of Cyril in the see of Alexandria, was appointed president by an intrigue, in enmity to Flavian, of Chrysaphius, who at that time swayed the imperial court. There hasten to Ephesus Juvenalis, bishop of Jerusalem, who was present at the former council, with AD 449 a great number of associate priests, and with him also Domnus, the successor of John at Antioch: and besides them, Julius, a bishop, who was the representative of Leo, bishop of the elder Rome. Flavian also was present with his associate bishops, an edict having been addressed by Theodosius to Elpidius, in these precise terms:

"Provided that those who had on the former occasion passed judgment on the most religious Archimandrite Eutyches, be present, but take no part in the proceedings, by abstaining from the functions of judges and awaiting the resolution of all the most holy fathers; inasmuch as their own previous decision is now a subject of inquisition."

In this council, the deposition of Eutyches is revoked by Dioscorus and his associates—as is contained in the acts—and that sentence is passed upon Flavian, and Eusebius, president of the church of Dorylæum. At the same time, Ibas, bishop of Edessa, is excommunicated; and Daniel, bishop of Carrhae, Irenæus of Tyre, and Aquilinus of Byblus, are deposed. Some measures were also taken on account of Sophronius, bishop of Constantina: and they depose Theodoret, bishop of Cyrus, and even Domnus of Antioch. What afterwards befell the last mentioned, I am not able to discover. After these proceedings the second council of Ephesus was dissolved.

CHAPTER XI

AN APOLOGY FOR DIFFERENCES OF OPINION AMONG CHRISTIANS.

And here let not any one of the deluded worshippers of idols presume to sneer, as if it were the business of succeeding councils to depose their predecessors, and to be ever devising some addition to the faith. For while we are endeavoring to trace the unutterable and unsearchable scheme of God's mercy to man, and to revere and exalt it to the utmost, our opinions are swayed in this or that direction: and with none of those who have been the authors of heresies among Christians, was blasphemy the first intention; nor did they fall from the truth in a desire to dishonor the Deity, but rather from an idea which each entertained, that he should improve upon his predecessors by upholding such and such doctrines.

Besides, all parties agree in a confession which embraces the essential points; for a Trinity is the single object of our worship, and unity the complex one of our glorification, and the Word, who is God begotten before the worlds, and became flesh by a second birth in mercy to the creature: and if new opinions have been broached on other points, these also have arisen from the freedom granted to our will by our Savior God, even on these subjects, in order that the holy catholic and apostolic church might be the more exercised in bringing opposing opinions into captivity to truth and piety, and arrive, at length, at one smooth and straight path. Accordingly the apostle says most distinctly: "There is need of heresies among you, that the approved ones may be manifested."[5] And here also, we have occasion to admire the unutterable wisdom of God, who said to the divine Paul, "My strength is made perfect in weakness."[6] For by the very causes by which the members of the church have been broken off, the true and pure doctrine has been more accurately established, and the catholic and apostolic church of God has attained amplification and exaltation to heaven.

But those who have been nurtured in Grecian error, having no desire to extol God or his tender care of men, were continually endeavoring to shake the opinions of their predecessors, and of each other rather devising gods upon gods, and assigning to them by express titles the tutelage of their own passions, in order that they might find an excuse for their own debaucheries by associating such deities with them. Thus, their supreme father of gods and men, under the form of a bird, shamelessly carried off the Phrygian boy; and as a reward of his vile service bestowed the cup, with leave to pledge him in an amorous draught, that they might with the nectar drink in their common shame. Besides innumerable other villainies, reprobated by the meanest of mankind, and transformations into every form of brutes, himself the most brutish of all, he becomes bi-sexually pregnant, if not in his belly yet in his thigh, that even this violation of nature might be fulfilled in his person: whence springing, the bi-sexual dithyrambic birth outraged either sex; author of drunkenness surfeit, and mad debauch, and all their fearful consequences. To this Ægis-wearer, this Thunderer, they attach, in spite of these majestic titles, the crime of parricide, universally regarded as the extremity of guilt; inasmuch as he dethroned Saturn who unhappily had begotten him.

Why need I also mention their consecration of fornication, over which they made Venus to preside, the shell-born Cyprian, abhorred chastity as an unhallowed and monstrous thing but delighted in fornication and all filthiness, and willed to be propitiated by them: in whose company Mars also suffers unseemly exposure, being, by the contrivance of Vulcan, made a spectacle and laughing-stock to the gods? Justly would one ridicule their phalli and ithyphalli, and phallagogia; their Priapus, and Pan, and the Eleusinian mysteries, which in one respect deserve praise, namely, that the sun was not allowed to see them, but they were condemned to dwell with darkness.

Leaving, then, the worshippers and the worshipped in their shame, let us urge our steed to the goal, and set forth, in compendious survey, the remaining transactions of the reign of Theodosius.

CHAPTER XII

CONDEMNATION OF THE NESTORIAN DOCTRINE BY THEODOSIUS.

Theodosius, then, issued a most pious constitution, which is included in the first book of what is termed the Code of Justinian, and is the third under the first title; in which, moved by heaven, he condemned, by all the votes, as the saying is, him to whom he had been long attached, as Nestorius himself writes, and placed him under anathema. The precise terms are as follow:

"Further we ordain, that those who favor the impious creed of Nestorius, or follow his unlawful doctrine, be ejected from the holy churches, if they be bishops or clerks; and if laics, be anathematized."

Other enactments were also promulgated by him relating to our religion, which show his burning zeal.

CHAPTER XIII

SIMEON THE STYLITE.

In these times flourished and became illustrious, Simeon, of holy and famous memory, who originated the contrivance of stationing himself on the top of a column, thereby occupying a spot of scarce two cubits in circumference. Domnus was then bishop of Antioch; and he, having visited Simeon, and being struck with the singularity of his position and mode of life, was desirous of more mystic intercourse. They met accordingly, and having consecrated the immaculate body, imparted to each other the life-giving communion. This man, endeavoring to realize in the flesh the existence of the heavenly hosts, sits himself above the concerns of earth, and, overpowering the downward tendency of man's nature, is intent upon things above: placed between earth and heaven, he holds communion with God, and unites with the angels in praising him; from earth, his intercessions on behalf of men, and from drawing down upon them the divine favor.

An account of his miracles has been written by one of those who were eye-witnesses, and an eloquent record by Theodoret, bishop of Cyrus: though they have omitted a circumstance in particular, the memory of which I found to be still retained by the inhabitants of the holy desert, and which I learnt from them as follows. When Simeon, that angel upon earth, that citizen in the flesh of the heavenly Jerusalem, had devised this strange and hitherto unknown walk, the inhabitants of the holy desert send a person to him, charged with an injunction to render a reason of this singular habitude, namely, why, abandoning the beaten path which the saints had trodden, he is pursuing another altogether unknown to mankind; and, further, that he should come down and travel the road of the elect fathers. They, at the same time, gave orders, that, if he should manifest perfect readiness to come down, liberty should be given him to follow out the course he had chosen, inasmuch as his compliance would be sufficient proof that under God's guidance he persevered in this his endurance: but that he should be dragged down by force, in case he should manifest repugnance, or be swayed by self-will, and refuse to be guided implicitly by the injunction.

When the person, thus deputed came and announced

the command of the fathers, and Simeon, in pursuance of the injunction, immediately put one foot forward, then he declared him free to fulfill his own course, saying, 'Be stout, and play the man: the post which thou hast chosen is from God.' This circumstance, which is omitted by those who have written about him, I have thus thought worthy of record.

In so great a measure had the power of divine grace taken possession of him, that, when Theodosius had issued a mandate, that the synagogues of which they had been previously deprived by the Christians, should be restored to the Jews of Antioch, he wrote to the emperor with so much freedom and vehement rebuke, as standing in awe of none but his own immediate sovereign, that Theodosius re-called his commands, and in every respect favored the Christians, even superseding the prefect who had suggested the measure. He further proceeded to prefer a request to this effect, to the holy and aerial martyr, that he would entreat and pray for him, and impart a share of his own peculiar benediction.

Simeon prolonged his endurance of this mode of life through fifty-six years, nine of which he spent in the first monastery, where he was instructed in divine knowledge and forty-seven in the Mandra, as it is termed; namely, ten in a certain nook; on shorter columns, seven; and thirty upon one of forty cubits. After his departure, his holy body was conveyed to Antioch, during the episcopate of Martyrius, and the reign of the emperor Leo, when AD 459 Ardabyrius was in command of the forces of the East, on which occasion the troops with a concourse of their followers and others, proceeded to the Mandra, and escorted the venerable body of the blessed Simeon, lest the inhabitants of the neighboring cities should muster and carry it off. In this manner, it was conveyed to Antioch, and attended during its progress by extraordinary prodigies. The emperor also demanded possession of the body; and the people of Antioch addressed to him a petition in deprecation of his purpose, in these terms: "Forasmuch as our city is without walls, for we have been visited in wrath by their fall, we brought hither the sacred body to be our wall and bulwark." Moved by these considerations, the emperor yielded to their prayer, and left them in possession of the venerable body.

It has been preserved nearly entire to my time: and, in company with many priests, I enjoyed the sight of his sacred head, in the episcopate of the famous Gregory, when Philippicus had requested that precious relics of saints might be sent to him for the protection of the Eastern armies. And, strange as is the circumstance, the hair of his head had not perished, but is in the same state of preservation as when he was alive and sojourning with mankind. The skin of his forehead, too, was wrinkled and indurated, but is nevertheless preserved, as well as the greater part of his teeth, except such as had been violently removed by the hands of faithful men, affording by their appearance an indication of the personal appearance and years of the man of God. Beside the head lies the iron collar to which, as the companion of its endurance, the famous body has imparted a share of its own divinely bestowed honors; for not even in death has Simeon been deserted by the loving iron. In this manner would I have detailed every particular, thereby benefiting both myself and my readers, had not Theodoret, as I said before, already performed the task more fully.

CHAPTER XIV

DESCRIPTION OF THE APPEARANCE OF A STAR NEAR THE COLUMN OF SIMEON.

Let me, however, add a record of another circumstance which I witnessed. I was desirous of visiting the precinct of this saint, distant nearly thirty stadia from Theopolis, and situated near the very summit of the mountain. The people of the country give it the title of Mandra, a name bequeathed to the spot, as

I suppose, by the holy Simeon, in respect of the discipline which he there had practiced. The ascent of the mountain is as much as twenty stadia. The temple constructed in the form of a cross, adorned with colonnades on the four sides. Beside the colonnades are arranged handsome columns of polished stone, sustaining a roof of considerable elevation; while the center is occupied by an unroofed court of the most excellent workmanship, where stands the pillar, of forty cubits, on which the incarnate angel upon earth spent his heavenly life. Adjoining the roof of the colonnades is a balustrade, termed by some persons windows, forming a fence towards both the before-mentioned court and the colonnades.

At the balustrade, on the left of the pillar, I saw, in company with all the people who were there assembled, while the rustics were performing dances round it, a very large and brilliant star, shooting along the whole balustrade, not merely once, twice, or thrice, but repeatedly; vanishing moreover, frequently, and again suddenly appearing: and this occurs only at the commemorations of the saint. There are also persons who affirm—and there is no reason to doubt the prodigy, considering the credibility of the vouchers, and the other circumstances which I actually witnessed—that they have a seen a resemblance of the saint's face flitting about here and there, with a long beard, and wearing a tiara, as was his habit.

Free ingress is allowed to men, who repeatedly compass the pillar with their beasts of burden: but the most scrupulous precaution is taken, for what reason I am unable to say, that no woman should enter the sacred building: but they obtain a view of the prodigy from the threshold without, since one of the doors is opposite to the star of rays.

CHAPTER XV

ISIDORE OF PELUSIUM
AND SYNESIUS OF CYRENE.

In the same reign Isidore was also conspicuous: "wide whose renown," according to the language of poetry; having become universally celebrated by deed and word. To such a degree did he waste his flesh by severe discipline, and feed his soul by elevating doctrine, as to pursue upon earth the life of angels, and be ever a living monument of monastic life and contemplation of God. Besides his numerous other writings, well stored with various profit, there are some addressed to the renowned Cyril; from which it appears that he flourished contemporary with the divine bishop.

And now, while endeavoring to give every attraction to my work, let me also bring upon the scene Synesius of Cyrene, whose memory will add an embellishment to my narrative. This Synesius, while possessed of every other kind of learning, carried the study of philosophy, in particular, to its highest pitch; so as to gain the admiration even of those Christians whose decision upon things which fall under their observation is not guided by favoring or adverse prejudice. They, accordingly, persuade him to resolve on partaking of the saving regeneration, and to take upon himself the yoke of the priesthood, while as yet he did not admit the doctrine of the resurrection, nor was inclined to hold that tenet; anticipating, with well-aimed conjecture, that this belief would be added to his other excellencies, since divine grace is never content to leave its work unfinished. Nor were they disappointed in their expectation: for his epistles, written after his accession to the priesthood, and composed with elegance and learning, as well as his discourse addressed to Theodosius himself, and whatever is extant of his valuable writings, sufficiently show how excellent and great a man he was.

CHAPTER XVI

TRANSLATION OF THE REMAINS OF IGNATIUS.

At the same period also took place the translation of the divine Ignatius, as is recorded, with other matters by John the rhetorician: who, having found a tomb, as he himself desired, in the bowels of the wild beasts, in the amphitheater of Rome, had, nevertheless through the preservation of the more solid bones, which were conveyed to Antioch, long reposed in what is called the cemetery: the good God having moved Theodosius to dignify the bearer of the name Theophorus with increased honors, and to dedicate a temple long ago devoted to the demons, and called by the inhabitants Tychæum, to the victorious martyr. Thus, what was formerly the shrine of Fortune, became a sanctuary and holy precinct for Ignatius, by depositing there his sacred remains, which were conveyed on a car through the city, attended by a solemn procession. From this event arose the celebration of a public festival, accompanied with rejoicings of the whole population; which has continued to our times and received increased magnificence at the hands of the prelate Gregory.

Such results were brought about by the conspiring agency of friends and foes while God was decreeing honor to the holy memories of the saints. For the impious Julian, that heaven-detested power, when the Daphnæan Apollo whose prophetic voice proceeded from the Castalian fount, could give no response to the emperor's consultation, since the holy Babylas, from his neighboring resting-place, restrained his utterance; was goaded on to be an unwilling instrument in honoring that saint by a translation; on which occasion was also erected to him, outside the city, a spacious temple, which has remained entire to the present day: the object of removal being that the demons might no longer be overawed in the pursuit of their own practices, the performance of which, as

23

is said, they had previously promised to Julian. Thus were events disposed by the providence of God, in his design that both the power of those who were dignified by martyrdom should be clearly manifested, and the sacred relics of the holy martyr should be transferred to sacred ground, and be honored with a noble precinct.

CHAPTER XVII

ATTILA KING OF THE HUNS. EARTHQUAKES.

During those times arose the celebrated war of Attila, king of the Scythians: the history of which has been written with great care and distinguished ability by Priscus the rhetorician, who details, in a very elegant narrative, his attacks on the eastern and western parts of the empire, how many and important cities he reduced, and the series of his achievements until he was removed from the world.

It was also in the reign of Theodosius that an extraordinary earthquake occurred, which threw all former ones into the shade, and extended, so to speak, over the whole world. Such was its violence, that many of the towers in different parts of the imperial city were overthrown and the long wall, as it is termed, of the Chersonese, was laid in ruins; the earth opened and swallowed up many villages; and innumerable other calamities happened both by land and sea. Several fountains became dry, and, on the other hand, large bodies of water were formed on the surface, where none existed before: entire trees were torn up by the roots and hurled aloft and mountains were suddenly formed by the accumulation of masses thrown up. The sea also cast up dead fish; many islands were submerged; and, again, ships were seen stranded by the retreat of the waters. At the same time Bithynia, the Hellespont, and either Phrygia suffered severely. This calamity prevailed for a considerable time, though the violence with which it commenced, did not continue, but abated by degrees until it entirely ceased.

CHAPTER XVIII
ANTIOCH EMBELLISHED BY DIFFERENT GOVERNORS.

In the course of the same period, Memnonius, Zoilus, and Callistus, were sent out by Theodosius to the government of Antioch, men who made our religion an object of marked honor. Memnonius also rebuilt from the foundation, in a beautiful and elaborate style, the edifice which we name Psephium, leaving an unroofed court in the center. Zoilus built the basilica which is situated on the south side of that of Rufinus and which has continued to bear his name to our times, although the structure itself has undergone changes from various casualties. Callistus, too, erected a noble and striking edifice, called both in former and present times the Basilica of Callistus, in front of the seats of justice, and opposite the forum where stand the splendid buildings which are the quarters of the military commanders. Subsequently, Anatolius, having been sent out as commander of the forces of the East, erects the basilica which bears his name, and embellishes it with every variety of material. The introduction of these matters, though beside my more immediate purpose will not offend the taste of the curious reader.

CHAPTER XIX
WARS DURING THE REIGN OF THEODOSIUS.

In the times of Theodosius, repeated revolts took place in Europe, during the reign of Valentinian at Rome. These were crushed by Theodosius, who sent out for that purpose large land and naval forces. He also so far quelled the insolence of the Persians, whose sovereign at that time was Isdigerdes, the father of Vararanes, or, as Socrates thinks, Vararanes himself, as to reduce them to solicit peace; which was granted, and lasted till the twelfth year of the reign of Anastasius. These transactions have been recorded by other writers, and have also been very elegantly epitomized by Eustathius of Epiphania, the Syrian, who wrote, besides, an account of the capture of Amida.

In that age, too, it is said that the poets Claudian and Cyrus flourished; and that Cyrus was elevated to the seat of highest dignity among the prefects, styled by our ancestors the prefect of the palace, and was also invested with the command of the forces of the West when the Vandals under Genseric had made themselves masters of Carthage.

CHAPTER XX

THE EMPRESS EUDOCIA.

Theodosius also espoused Eudocia, who had previously participated in the saving baptism; an Athenian by birth, and distinguished by poetic skill and beauty of person; through the offices of his sister, the princess Pulcheria. By her he had a daughter Eudoxia, whom, when she had reached a marriageable age, the emperor Valentinian afterwards espoused; for which purpose he made a voyage from the elder Rome to the city of Constantine.

At a subsequent period, when Eudocia was pursuing a journey to the holy city of Christ our God, she also visits this place; and concluded an address to our people with the following verse, "'Tis from your blood I proudly trace my line:"[7] in allusion to the colonies which were sent hither from Greece. Of these, if any one is curious to know the particulars, an elaborate account has been given by Strabo, the geographer, Phlegon, and Diodorus Siculus, as well as by Arrian and Pisander the poet, and, besides, by the distinguished sophists, Ulpian, Libanius, and Julian. On this occasion, the sons of the Antiochenes honored her with a skillfully executed statue in brass, which has been preserved even to our times. At her suggestion, Theodosius considerably enlarges the bounds of the city, by extending the circuit of the wall as far as the gate which leads to the suburb of Daphne: of which those who are disposed, may assure themselves by visible proof; for the whole wall may be still traced, since the remains afford a sufficient guidance to the eye. Some, however, say that the elder Theodosius extended the wall. He gave, besides, two hundred pounds' weight of gold for the restoration of the baths of Valens, which had been partially burnt.

CHAPTER XXI

VISITS OF EUDOCIA TO JERUSALEM. ASCETICS.

From this city Eudocia proceeds on two occasions to Jerusalem; but on account of what circumstances, or with what object in the first instance, must be gathered through those writers who have treated the subject, although they do not appear to me to give true accounts. At all events, when visiting the holy city of Christ, she did many things for the honor of our Savior God, even so far as to erect holy monasteries, and what are termed lauræ.

In these places the mode of life is different, but the discipline of each terminates in the same devout object. For those who live together in companies are still not under the influence of any of those things which weigh down to the earth, since they possess no gold: but why should I say gold when no article of even dress or food is the sole property of any one among them, but the gown or vest which one is now wearing, another presently puts on, so that the clothing of all appears to belong to one, and that of one to all. A common table also is set before them, not delicately furnished with meats or any other dainties, but supplied with fare of herbs and pulse, and that only in sufficient quantity to sustain life. They maintain common supplications to God throughout the day and night, to such a degree distressing themselves, so galling themselves by their severe service, as to seem, in a manner, tombless corpses. They also frequently practice superadditions, as they are called, namely, by maintaining their fastings for two or three days; and some on the fifth day, or even later, scarcely allow themselves a portion of necessary food. On the other hand, there is a class who pursue a contrary course, and individually seclude themselves in chambers of so limited a height and width, that they can neither stand upright nor lie down at ease, confining their existence to "dens and caves of the earth," as says the apostle.[8]

Some, too, take up their dwelling with the wild beasts, and in untracked recesses of the ground; and thus offer their supplications to God. Another mode has also been devised, one which reaches to the utmost extent of resolution and endurance: for transporting themselves to a scorched wilderness, and covering only those parts which nature requires to be concealed, both men and women leave the rest of their persons exposed both to excessive frosts and scorching blasts, regardless alike of heat and cold. They, moreover, cast off the ordinary food of mankind, and feed upon the produce of the ground, whence they are termed Grazers; allowing themselves no more than is barely sufficient to sustain life. In consequence, they at length became assimilated to wild beasts, with their outward form altogether disfigured, and their mind in a state no longer fitted for intercourse with their species, whom they even shun when they see them; and, on being pursued, contrive to escape, favored either by their swiftness of foot, or by places difficult of access.

I will mention still another class, which had almost escaped recollection, though it bears away the preeminence from all others. Its numbers are very small; but still there are persons, who, when by virtue they have attained to a condition exempt from passion, return to the world. In the midst of the stir, by plainly intimating that they are indifferent to those who view them with amazement, they thus trample under foot vain-glory, the last garment, according to the wise Plato, which it is the nature of the soul to cast off. By similar means they study the art of apathy in eating, practicing it even, if need be, with the petty retailers of victuals. They also constantly frequent the public baths, mostly mingling and bathing with women, since they have attained to such an ascendancy over their passions, as to possess dominion over nature, and neither by sight, touch, or even embracing of the female, to relapse into their natural condition; it being their desire to be men among men, and women among women, and to participate in both sexes.

In short, by a life thus all excellent and divine, virtue exercises a sovereignty in opposition to nature, establishing her own laws, so as not to allow them to partake to satiety in any necessary. Indeed, their own rule enjoins them to hunger and thirst, and clothe the body only so far as necessity requires: and their mode of life is balanced by opposite scales, so accurately poised, that they are unconscious of any tendency to motion, though arising from strongly antagonist forces; for opposing principles are, in the case, mingled to such a degree, by the power of divine grace combining and again severing things that are incongruous, that life and death dwell together in them, things opposed to each other in nature and in circumstances: for where passion enters, they must be dead and entombed; where prayer to God is required, they must display vigor of body and energy of spirit, though the flower of life be past. Thus with them are the two modes of life combined, so as to be constantly living with a total renunciation of the flesh, and at the same time mingling with the living; both applying remedies to their bodies, and presenting to God the cries of suppliants, and in all other respects fully maintaining a practice in accordance with their former mode of life, except as regards restriction in intercourse and place: on the contrary, they listen to all and associate with all. They also practice a long and continuous series of kneelings and risings, their earnestness alone serving to reinvigorate their years and self-inflicted weakness; being, as it were, fleshless athletes, bloodless wrestlers, esteeming fasting as a varied and luxurious feast, and the utmost abstinence from food a completely furnished table. On the other hand, whenever a stranger visits them, even at early dawn, they welcome him with generous entertainment, devising another form of fasting in eating against their will.

Hence the marvel, how far the pittance on which they subsist falls short of a sufficient allowance of food; foes of their own desires and of nature, but devoted to the wills of those around them, in order that fleshly enjoyment may be constantly expelled, and the soul, diligently selecting and maintaining whatever is most seemly and pleasing to God, may alone bear sway: happier in their mode of existence here, happier in their departure hence, on which they are ever intent impatient to behold Him whom they desire.

CHAPTER XXII

BUILDINGS ERECTED BY EUDOCIA.
ACCESSION OF MARCIAN.

After having conversed with many persons of this description, and founded, as I have already said, many such seats of contemplation, and, besides, restored the walls of Jerusalem, the consort of Theodosius also erected a very large sanctuary, conspicuous for elevation and beauty, in honor of Stephen, the first of deacons and martyrs, distant less than a stadium from Jerusalem. Here her own remains were deposited, when she had departed to the unfading life.

When Theodosius had subsequently, or, as some think, before Eudocia, departed the sovereignty which he had administered for eight and thirty years, the most excellent Marcian is invested with the empire of the Romans. The sequel of my history shall very clearly set forth the transactions of his reign over the East, while the heavenly impulse bestows its own kindly aid.

NOTES

1. The city of Antioch was renamed Theopolis—City of God—after the catastrophic earthquake of AD 526. See Book IV, Chapter V and VI. Antioch and Theopolis are used interchangably by Evagrius throughout his history.
2. The term "libel" in this context should be understood as testimony presented to an ecclesiastical court, and not in the sense of defamatory statements. Whitby translates the term as "depositions" (Whitby, p. 106).
3. 1 Samuel 2:30.
4. Thucydides. B. ii. c. 45.
5. 1 Corinthians 11:19.
6. 2 Corinthians 12:9.
7. Hom. II. vi. 211.
8. Hebrews 11:38.

THE SECOND BOOK

CHAPTER I

FORTUNES AND CHARACTER OF MARCIAN.

The transactions of the time of Theodosius have been embraced in the preceding book. Let me now introduce upon the scene Marcian, the renowned emperor of the Romans, and in so doing, first recount who and whence he was, and by what means he won the imperial power: and having done this, let me record the occurrences of his reign in the order of time.

AD 450

Marcian, as has been recorded by many other writers, and in particular by Priscus, the rhetorician, was by birth a Thracian, and the son of a military man. In his desire to follow his father's mode of life, he had set out for Philippopolis, where he could be enrolled in the legions, and on the road sees the body of a person recently slain, lying exposed upon the ground. On going up to it—for, besides the excellence of his other virtues, he was singularly compassionate—he commiserated the occurrence, and suspended his journey for some time, from a desire to discharge the due offices to the dead. Some persons, observing the circumstance, reported it to the authorities at Philippopolis, and they proceeded to apprehend Marcian, and interrogated him respecting the murder and when, through the prevalence of conjecture and mere probability over truth and asseveration of innocence, he was upon the point of suffering the punishment of guilt, a providential interposition suddenly brings into their hands the real criminal, who, by forfeiting his own head as the penalty of the deed, procures an acquittance of the head of Marcian.

After this unexpected escape, he presents himself to one of the military bodies stationed in the place, with the intention of enlistment. Struck with the singularity of his fortunes, and with reason concluding that he would arrive at power and preeminent distinction, they gladly admitted him, and that too without placing him, according to military rule, lowest on the roll; but they assigned to him the grade of a lately deceased soldier, named Augustus, by inscribing in the list, Marcian, called also Augustus. Thus did his name anticipate the style of our sovereigns, who assume the title of Augustus on attaining the purple. It was as if the name refused to abide on him without its appropriate rank, and, on the other hand, the rank was not ambitious of another name for the augmentation of its style: and thus arose an identity of his personal and titular appellations, since his dignity and his name found an expression in the same term.

Another circumstance also occurred, which might serve as a prognostic of imperial power being destined to Marcian. When serving under Aspar against the Vandals, he was one of many who fell into their hands on the total defeat of that general; and, on the demand of Genseric to see the prisoners, was dragged with the rest along the plain. When the whole body was collected, Genseric sat in an upper chamber, surveying with delight the numbers that had been taken. As the time wore on, they pursued each his own inclination, for the guard had, at the order of Genseric, released them from their bonds; and while they accordingly disposed of themselves each in his several way, Marcian laid himself down upon the ground to sleep in the sun, which was shining with unusual heat for the season of the year. An eagle, however, poising his flight above him, and directly intercepting the sun as with a cloud, thus produced a shade and its consequent refreshment, to the amazement of Genseric, who, rightly presaging the future, sent for Marcian, and liberated him, having previously bound him by solemn oaths, that on attaining the imperial power he would maintain faithfully the rights of treaty towards the Vandals, and not commence hostilities against them; and Procopius records, that Marcian observed these conditions. But let us leave this digression, and return to my subject.

Marcian was pious towards God, and just towards those under his rule; regarding as wealth neither treasured stores nor the revenue of imposts, but only the means of providing relief to the needy, and to the wealthy the security of their possessions. He was dreaded, not in the infliction of punishment, but only by its anticipation. On this account he received the sovereignty not as an inheritance, but as the prize of virtue, conferred by the unanimous voice both of the senate and men of all ranks, at the suggestion of Pulcheria, whom he also espoused as his partner in the imperial dignity, though she still remained a virgin to old age. These transactions took place without a previous ratification of the choice by Valentinian, the emperor of Rome, who, however, accorded his approval to the virtues of the person elected. It was further the desire of Marcian, that an undivided service should be offered up by all to God, by uniting in pious concord the tongues which the arts of impiety had confounded, and that the Deity should be honored by one and the same doxology.

CHAPTER II

COUNCIL OF CHALCEDON SUMMONED BY MARCIAN.

While entertaining these intentions, the emperor is addressed both by the legates of Leo, bishop of the elder Rome, who alleged that Dioscorus had, during the second council of Ephesus, refused to receive the epistle of Leo, containing a formula of the true doctrine and also by those who had been contumeliously treated by Dioscorus, entreating that their case might be submitted to the decision of a synod. But Eusebius, who had been president of the church of Dorylæum, was especially urgent, and affirmed that both himself and Flavian had been deposed by the intrigues of Chrysaphius, the minister of Theodosius, because, in reply to his demand of an offering in gold, Flavian had, in acknowledgment of his own appointment, sent the sacred vessels to shame him; and also that Chrysaphius made a near approach to Eutyches in erroneous doctrine. He also said, that Flavian had even been brought to a miserable end by being thrust and trampled on by Dioscorus himself.

These circumstances caused the synod at Chalcedon to be assembled; for which purpose the bearers of missives were despatched, and the prelates in all quarters were summoned by pious letters. The place named was, in the first instance, Nicæa; and, accordingly, Leo, the president of Rome, on writing an epistle respecting Paschasianus, Lucentius, and others, whom he had sent as his representatives, inscribed it to the council assembled at Nicæa. It was, however, subsequently convened at Chalcedon in Bithynia.

Zacharias, the rhetorician, influenced by partiality, says that Nestorius was also fetched from his place of exile: but this is disproved by the circumstance, that Nestorius was generally anathematized by the members of the synod. And Eustathius, bishop of Berytus, clearly establishes the point, when writing in the following terms to John, a bishop, and another John, a presbyter, respecting the matters agitated in the assembly. "Those who were in quest of the remains of Nestorius, again presenting themselves, clamorously demanded of the synod, why the saints are anathematized: so that the emperor indignantly ordered the guards to drive them far from the place." How then Nestorius was summoned when he had departed from the world, I am unable to say.

CHAPTER III

DESCRIPTION OF THE CHURCH OF ST. EUPHEMIA.

The place of meeting was the sacred precinct of Euphemia, the martyr, situated in the district of Chalcedon in Bithynia, and distant not more than two stadia from the Bosphorus. The site is a beautiful spot, of so gentle an ascent, that those who are on their way to the temple, are not aware of their immediate approach, but suddenly find themselves within the sanctuary on elevated ground; so that, extending their gaze from a commanding position, they can survey the level surface of the plain spread out beneath them, green with herbage, waving with corn, and beautified with every kind of tree; at the same time including within their range woody mountains, towering gracefully or boldly swelling, as well as parts of the sea under various aspects: here, where the winds do not reach them, the still waters, with their dark blue tint, sweetly playing with gentle ripple on the beach; there wildly surging, and sweeping back the sea-weeds and the lighter shell-fish with the recoil of its waves. Directly opposite is Constantinople: and thus the beauty of the site is enhanced by the view of so vast a city. The holy place consists of three immense buildings. One is open to the sky, including a court of great extent, and embellished on all sides with columns; and next to it another, nearly resembling it in its length, breadth, and columns, and differing from it only in being roofed. On the north side of this, facing the East, is a round building, skillfully terminated in a dome, and surrounded in the interior with columns of uniform materials and size. These support a gallery under the same roof, so contrived, that those who are disposed, may thence both supplicate the martyr and be present at the mysteries. Within the domed building, towards the Eastern part, is a splendid enclosure, where are preserved the sacred remains of the martyr in a long coffin (it is distinguished by some persons by the term "long") of silver, skillfully worked.

The wonders which have at certain times been wrought by the holy martyr, are manifest to all Christians. For frequently she has appeared in a dream to the bishops of the city from time to time, and even to certain persons whose lives have been otherwise distinguished, and has bid them visit her and gather a vintage at her sanctuary. When such an occurrence has been ascertained by the sovereigns, the patriarch, and the city, they visit the temple, both those who sway the scepter, and those who are invested with sacred and civil offices, as well as the whole multitude, desirous to partake in the mysteries. Accordingly, the president of the church of Constantinople, with his attendant priests, enters, in sight of the public, the sanctuary where the already-mentioned sacred body is deposited. There is an aperture in the left side of the coffin, secured with small doors, through which they introduce a sponge attached to an iron rod, so as to reach the sacred relics and after turning it round, they draw it out, covered with stains and clots of blood. On witnessing this, all the people bend in worship, giving glory to God. So great has been the quantity of blood thus extracted, that both the pious sovereigns and the assembled priests, as well as the congregated people, all share in a liberal distribution, and portions are sent to those of the faithful who desire them, in every place under the sun. The clots also are permanent, neither does the appearance of the sacred blood undergo any change.

These divine manifestations occur not at the recurrence of any definite period, but according as the life of the prelate or gravity of manners calls for them. Accordingly it is said, that when the governor of the church is a person reverend and remarkable for virtues, the marvel occurs with peculiar frequency; but when such is not his character, such divine operations are rarely displayed. I will, however, mention a circumstance which suffers no interruption depending on lapse of time or seasonable occasion, nor yet is vouchsafed with a distinction between the faithful and infidels, but to all indiscriminately. Whenever any person approaches the spot where is deposited the precious coffin in which are the holy relics, he is filled with an odor surpassing in sweetness every perfume with which mankind are acquainted, for it resembles neither the mingled fragrance of the meadows, nor that which is exhaled from the sweetest substances, nor is it such as perfumer could prepare: but it is of a peculiar and surpassing kind, of itself sufficiently indicating the virtue of its source.

CHAPTER IV

COUNCIL OF CHALCEDON.

This was, then, the place of meeting of the before-mentioned synod; at which the bishops Paschasinus and Lucentius, and the presbyter Boniface, were the representatives of Leo, archpriest of the elder Rome; there being present Anatolius president of Constantinople, Dioscorus, bishop of   AD 451 Alexandria, Maximus of Antioch, and Juvenalis of Jerusalem: on whom attended both their associate priests, and those who held the places of highest rank in the most excellent senate.

To the latter the representatives of Leo alleged, that Dioscorus ought not to be seated with themselves; for such, they said, were their instructions from their bishop: as also that they would withdraw from the church, if they should be unable to maintain this point. In reply to the question of the senators, what were the charges against Dioscorus, they stated, that he ought himself to render an account of his own decision, since he had unduly assumed the character of a judge. After this statement had been made, and Dioscorus, according to a resolution of the senate, had taken his seat in the center, Eusebius demanded, in the following words, that the petition should be read which he had presented to the sovereign power: "I have been wronged by Dioscorus; the faith has been wronged: the bishop Flavian was murdered, and, together with myself, unjustly deposed by him. Give directions that my petition be read." When the matter had been discussed, the petition was allowed to be read: it was couched in the following terms.

"To our Christ-loving and most religious and pious sovereigns, Flavius Valentinianus, and Flavius Marcianus, the petition of Eusebius, the very humble bishop of Dorylæum, who now pleads on behalf of himself and the orthodox faith, and the sainted Flavian, formerly bishop of Constantinople. It is the aim of your majesty to exercise a providential care of all your subjects, and stretch forth a protecting hand to all who are suffering wrong, and to those especially who are invested with the priesthood; for by this means service is rendered to God, from whom you have received the bestowal of supremacy and power over all regions under the sun. Inasmuch, then, as the Christian faith and we have suffered many outrages at the hands of Dioscorus, the most reverent bishop of the great city of the Alexandrians, we address ourselves to your piety in pursuance of our rights.

"The circumstances of the case are as follow:— the synod lately held at the metropolitan city of the Ephesians—would that it had never met, nor the world been thereby filled with mischiefs and tumult—the excellent Dioscorus, regarding neither the principle of justice nor the fear of God, sharing also in the opinions and feelings of the visionary and heretical Eutyches, though unsuspected by the multitude of being such as he afterwards showed himself, took occasion of the charge advanced by me against his fellow in doctrine, Eutyches, and the decision given by the sainted bishop Flavian, and having gathered a disorderly rabble, and procured an overbearing influence by bribes, made havoc, as far as lay in his power, of the pious religion of the orthodox, and established the erroneous doctrine of Eutyches the monk, which had from the first been repudiated by the holy fathers.

"Since, then, his aggressions against the Christian faith and us are of no trifling magnitude, we beseech and supplicate your majesty to issue your commands to the same most reverent bishop Dioscorus, to defend himself against our allegations; namely, when the record of the acts which Dioscorus procured against us, shall be read before the holy synod; on the ground of which we are able to show that he is estranged from the orthodox faith, that he strengthened a heresy utterly impious, that he wrongfully deposed and has cruelly outraged us. And this we will do on the issuing of your divine and reverend mandates to the holy and universal synod of the bishops, highly beloved of God, to the effect, that they should give a formal hearing to the matters which concern both us and the before-mentioned Dioscorus, and refer all the transactions to the decision of your piety, as shall seem fit to your immortal supremacy. If we obtain this our request, we shall ever pray for your everlasting rule, most divine sovereigns."

In the next place, at the joint request of Dioscorus and Eusebius, the acts of the second council of Ephesus were publicly read, the particulars of which, as being lengthy, and at the same time embraced by the detail of the proceedings at Chalcedon, I have subjoined to the present book of the history, that I might not seem prolix to those who are eager to be brought to the end of the transactions; thereby leaving to such as are desirous of minute acquaintance with every particular, the means of leisurely consultation and an accurate conception of the whole. By way of a cursory statement of the more important points, I mention that Dioscorus was convicted of having suppressed the epistle of Leo, bishop of the elder Rome; and further, of having enacted the deposition of Flavian, bishop of new Rome, in the space of a single day, and procured the subscriptions of the assembled prelates to a blank paper, represented as containing the form of the deposition. Upon these grounds, the senators decreed as follows:

41

"Of points relating to the orthodox and catholic faith, we are agreed that a more exact inquiry should take place before a fuller assembly of the council, at its next meeting. But inasmuch as it has been shown, from examination of the acts and decrees, and from the oral testimony of the presidents of that synod, who admit that themselves were in error, and the deposition was void, that Flavian of pious memory, and the most reverent Bishop Eusebius, were convicted of no error concerning the faith and were wrongfully deposed, it seems to us, according to God's good pleasure, to be a just proceeding if approved by our most divine and pious sovereign, that Dioscorus, the most reverent bishop of Alexandria; Juvenalis, the most reverent bishop of Jerusalem; Thalassius, the most reverent bishop of Cæsarea, in Cappadocia; Eusebius, the most reverent bishop of Ancyra; Eustathius, the most reverent bishop of Berytus; and Basilius, the most reverent bishop of Seleucia, in Isauria; who exercised sway and precedency in that synod; should be subjected to the selfsame penalty, by suffering at the hands of the holy synod deprivation of their episcopal dignity, according to the canons; whatever is consequent hereupon, being submitted to the cognizance of the emperor's sacred supremacy."

On the presentation of libels against Dioscorus at the next meeting of the council, containing charges of slander and extortion, and his refusal, for certain alleged reasons, to appear, after a twice and thrice repeated summons, the representatives of Leo, bishop of the elder Rome, made the following declaration:

"The aggressions committed by Dioscorus, lately bishop of the great city Alexandria, in violation of canonical order and the constitution of the church, have been clearly proved by the investigations at the former meeting, and the proceedings of today. For, not to mention the mass of his offenses, he did, on his own authority, uncanonically admit to communion his partisan Eutyches, after having been canonically deprived by his own bishop, namely, our sainted father and archbishop Flavian; and this before he sat in council with the other bishops at Ephesus. To them, indeed, the holy see granted pardon for the transactions of which they were not the deliberate authors, and they have hitherto continued obedient to the most holy archbishop Leo, and the body of the holy and universal synod; on which account he also admitted them into communion with him, as being his fellows in faith. Whereas Dioscorus has continued to maintain a haughty carriage, on account of those very circumstances over which he ought to have bewailed and humbled himself to the earth. Moreover, he did not even allow the epistle to be read which the blessed pope Leo had addressed to Flavian, of holy memory; and that too, notwithstanding he was repeatedly exhorted thereto by the bearers, and had promised with an oath to that effect.

The result of the epistle not being read, has been to fill the most holy churches throughout the world with scandals and mischief. Notwithstanding, however, such presumption, it was our purpose to deal mercifully with him as regards his past impiety, as we had done to the other bishops, although they had not held an equal judicial authority with him. But inasmuch as he has, by his subsequent conduct, overshot his former iniquity, and has presumed to pronounce excommunication against Leo, the most holy and religious archbishop of great Rome; since, moreover, on the presentation of a paper full of grievous charges against him to the holy and great synod, he refused to appear, though once, twice, and thrice canonically summoned by the bishops, pricked no doubt by his own conscience; and since he has unlawfully given reception to those who had been duly deposed by different synods; he has thus, by variously trampling upon the laws of the church, given his own verdict against himself. Wherefore Leo, the most blessed and holy archbishop of the great and elder Rome, has, by the agency of ourselves and the present synod, in conjunction with the thrice-blessed and all honored

43

Peter, who is the rock and basis of the Catholic church, and the foundation of the orthodox faith, deprived him of the episcopal dignity, and severed him from every priestly function. Accordingly, this holy and great synod decrees the provisions of the canons on the aforesaid Dioscorus."

After the ratification of these measures by the synod, and the transaction of some other matters, those who had been deposed together with Dioscorus, were reinstated, at the request of the synod and the assent of the imperial government; and, after some further transactions, a definition of faith was announced in these precise words: "Our Lord Jesus Christ, while confirming the knowledge of the faith in his disciples, said, 'My peace I give to you; my peace I leave to you;' to the purpose, that no one should differ from his neighbor in the doctrines of piety, but should accord in publishing the declaration of the truth."

After the reading of the holy Nicene creed, and also that of the hundred and fifty holy fathers, they subjoined as follows: "This wise and salutary symbol of divine grace is indeed sufficient for the perfect knowledge and confirmation of godliness; for, concerning the Father, and the Son, and the Holy Spirit, its teaching is plain and complete, and it sufficiently suggests the incarnation of the Lord to those who receive it faithfully. But since the enemies of the truth are endeavoring to subvert its doctrine by heresies of their own, and have given birth to certain empty speeches, some daring to pervert the mystery of the economy which the Lord bore for our sakes, and rejecting the term 'Mother of God,' in the case of the Virgin; others introducing a confusion and commixture of substance, and inconsiderately moulding into one the natures of the flesh and of the Godhead, and by such confusion producing the monstrous notion of passibility in the divine nature of the Only-begotten; for this reason the present great and universal holy synod, from a desire to preclude every device of theirs against the truth, and to maintain the hitherto unshaken declaration of doctrine, has determined primarily that the creed of the three hundred and eighteen holy fathers shall be indefeasible; and, on account of those who impugn the Holy Spirit, it ratifies the doctrine delivered subsequently concerning the substance of the Spirit by the hundred and fifty fathers, who assembled in the imperial city, and by them promulgated universally, not as though they were supplying some defect on the part of their predecessors, but were more clearly setting forth, by expressly recorded testimony, their notion respecting the Holy Spirit, in opposition to those who endeavored to annul His prerogative.

"In respect to those who have dared to corrupt the mystery of the economy, and with shameless wantonness to represent Him who was born of the holy Virgin as a mere man, the council has adopted the synodic epistles of the blessed Cyril, pastor of the church of the Alexandrians, addressed to Nestorius and the prelates of the East in refutation of the madness of Nestorius, and for the instruction of those who with pious zeal are desirous of being impressed with a due conception of the saving symbol. To these the council has not without reason appended, in order to the confirmation of the true doctrines, the epistle of the president of the great and elder Rome, which the most blessed and holy archbishop Leo addressed to the sainted archbishop Flavian, for the overthrow of the evil design of Eutyches; as being in agreement with the confession of the mighty Peter, and forming with it a monument of concurrent testimony against the maintainers of pernicious opinions; for it boldly confronts those who endeavor to dissever the mystery of the economy into a duality of sons; it expels from the congregation of the holy rites, those who presume to affirm that the Godhead of the Only-begotten is passible; and opposes those who imagine a mixture or confusion in respect of the two natures of Christ. It also ejects such as fondly fancy that the form of a servant which He assumed from our own nature, was of a heavenly or any other substance; and it anathematizes those who fable a resolution into one, at their union, of two previous natures of the Lord.

"Following, accordingly, the holy fathers, we confess one and the same Son, our Lord Jesus Christ, and we all with one voice declare him to be the same time perfect in Godhead, and perfect in manhood, very God, and at the same time very man, consisting of a reasonable soul and a body, being consubstantial with the Father as respects his Godhead, and at the same time consubstantial with ourselves as respects his manhood; resembling us in all things, independently of sin; begotten, before the ages, of the Father, according to his Godhead, but born, in the last of the days, of Mary, the virgin and mother of God, for our sakes and for our salvation; being one and the same Jesus Christ, Son, Lord, Only-begotten, made known in two natures without confusion, without conversion, without severance, without separation, inasmuch as the difference of the natures is in no way annulled by their union, but the peculiar essence of each nature is rather preserved, and conspires in one person and one subsistence, not as though he were parted or severed into two persons, but is one and the same Son, Only-begotten, Divine Word, Lord Jesus Christ, as the prophets declared concerning Him, and Christ himself has fully instructed us, and the symbol of the fathers has conveyed to us.

Since, then, these matters have been defined by us with all accuracy and diligence, the holy and universal synod has determined that no one shall be at liberty to put forth another faith, whether in writing, or by framing, or devising, or teaching it to others. And that those who shall presume to frame, or publish, or teach another faith, or to communicate another symbol to those who are disposed to turn to the knowledge of the truth from heathenism or Judaism, or any other sect—that they, if they be bishops or clerks, shall suffer deprivation, the bishops of their episcopal, the clerks of their clerical office; and if monks or laics, shall be anathematized."

After the reading of the formula, the emperor Marcian visited Chalcedon, and attended the synod, and, having delivered an harangue, again took his departure. Juvenalis also and Maximus arranged on mutual terms the matters relating to their own provinces, and Theodoret and Ibas were reinstated. Other matters were also mooted; an account of which, as I have already said, is subjoined to this history. It was also determined that the see of New Rome, while ranking second to that of Old Rome, should take precedence of all others.

CHAPTER V

TUMULT AT ALEXANDRIA—AND AT JERUSALEM.

In addition to these transactions, Dioscorus is sentenced to reside at Gangra in Paphlagonia, and Proterius is appointed to the see of Alexandria by a general vote of the synod. On his taking possession of his see, a very great and intolerable tumult arose among the people, who were roused into a storm against conflicting opinions; for some, as is likely in such cases, desired the restoration of Dioscorus, while others resolutely upheld Proterius, so as to give rise to many irremediable mischiefs. Thus Priscus, the rhetorician, recounts, that he arrived at Alexandria from the Thebaid, and that he saw the populace advancing in a mass against the magistrates: AD 451 that when the troops attempted to repress the tumult, they proceeded to assail them with stones, and put them to flight, and on their taking refuge in the old temple of Serapis, carried the place by assault, and committed them alive to the flames: that the emperor, when informed of these events, despatched two thousand newly levied troops, who made so favorable a passage, as to reach Alexandria on the sixth day; and that thence resulted still more alarming consequences, from the license of the soldiery towards the wives and daughters of the Alexandrians: that, subsequently, the people, being assembled in the hippodrome, entreated Florus, who was the military commandant, as well as the civil governor, with such urgency as to procure terms for themselves, in the distribution of provisions, of which he had deprived them, as well as the privileges of the baths and spectacles, and all others from which, on account of their turbulence, they had been debarred: that, at his suggestion, Florus presented himself to the people, and pledged himself to that effect, and by this means stopped the sedition for a time.

Nor did even the wilderness in the neighborhood of Jerusalem preserve its tranquillity, unvisited by this commotion. For there arrived in Palestine some of the monks who had been present at the council, but were disposed to harbor designs in opposition to it; and by lamenting the betrayal of the faith, exerted themselves to fan into a flame the monastic body. And when Juvenalis, after obtaining restitution to his see, had been compelled to return to the imperial city, by the violence of the party who claimed the right to supersede and anathematize in their own province, those who, as we have already mentioned, were opposed to the acts of the council of Chalcedon, assembled in the church of the Resurrection, and appointed Theodosius, who had especially caused confusion in the council, and been the first to bring a report of its proceedings, and respecting whom, at a subsequent period, the monks of Palestine alleged, in letters to Alcison, that having been convicted of malpractices in relation to his own bishop, he had been expelled from his monastery: and that at Alexandria he had impugned the conduct of Dioscorus, and, after having been severely scourged as a seditious person, had been conveyed round the city on a camel, as is usual with malefactors. To him many of the cities of Palestine made application, with a view to the ordination of bishops. Among these was Peter the Iberian; to whom was committed the episcopal helm of the city called Majumas, in the neighborhood of Gaza.

On being informed of these proceedings, Marcian, in the first place, commands Theodosius to be conveyed near his own person, and sends Juvenalis to rectify the past, with an injunction that all who had been ordained by Theodosius should be ejected. Many sad occurrences followed the arrival of Juvenalis, while either party indulged in whatever proceedings their anger suggested.

Such was the device of the envious and God-hating demon in the change of a single letter, that, while in reality the one expression was completely inductive of the notion of the other, still with the generality the discrepancy between them was held to be considerable, and the ideas conveyed by them to be clearly in diametric opposition, and exclusive of each other: whereas he who confesses Christ in two natures, clearly affirms Him to be from two; inasmuch as by confessing Christ at once in Godhead and manhood, he asserts His consistence from Godhead and manhood; and, on the other hand, the position of one who affirms His origin from two natures, is completely inclusive of His existence in two, inasmuch as he who affirms Christ to be from Godhead and manhood, confesses His existence in Godhead and manhood, since there is no conversion of the flesh into Godhead, nor a transition of the Godhead into flesh, from which substances arises the ineffable union. So that in this case by the expression, "from two natures," is aptly suggested the thought of the expression, "in two," and conversely; nor can there be a severance of the terms, this being an instance where a representation of the whole is afforded, not merely by its origin from component parts, but, as a further and distinct means, by its existence in them. Yet, nevertheless, persons have so taken up the idea of the marked distinction of the terms, either from a habit of thought respecting the glory of God, or by the inclination forestalling the judgment, as to be reckless of death in any shape, rather than acknowledge the real state of the case; and hence arose the occurrences which I have described. Such then was the state of these matters.

CHAPTER VI

DROUGHT, FAMINE, AND PESTILENCE
IN ASIA MINOR.

About the same time there was also a drought in Phrygia, Galatia, Cappadocia, and Cilicia: and, from want of ordinary necessaries, the inhabitants had recourse to unwholesome food, which further gave rise to pestilence. The change of food caused disease; excessive inflammation produced a swelling of the body, followed by loss of sight, and attended with a cough, and death took place on the third day. For a time no relief could be devised for the pestilence; but all-preserving Providence vouchsafed to the survivors a remedy for the famine, by raining down food in the unproductive year, in the same way as what was termed manna upon the Israelites; and, during the succeeding year, by willing that the fruits of the earth should be matured spontaneously. The spread of these calamities included also Palestine and innumerable other districts, making, as it were, a circuit of the earth.

CHAPTER VII

DEATH OF THE EMPEROR VALENTINIAN.
ROME TAKEN. SUCCESSORS OF VALENTINIAN.

During the progress of these events in the East, Ætius meets with a miserable end at Old Rome, and Valentinian, the emperor of the West, is slain, together with Heraclius, by some of the guards of Ætius, at the instigation of Maximus, who afterwards assumed the sovereignty, and who conspired against them because Valentinian had violated his wife. This Maximus forces Eudoxia, the wife of Valentinian, into a marriage with himself; and she, justly regarding the transaction as an outrage and altogether monstrous, determined to set, as the saying is, all upon a cast, on account of the wrong she had suffered both in the person of her husband and the infringement of her liberty: for a woman, jealous of her chastity, is unscrupulous and implacable if she has suffered defilement, especially by one through whose means she has been deprived of her husband. Accordingly, she sends to Genseric in Africa, and by considerable presents, as well as by holding out confident expectations of the future, induces him to make a sudden descent upon the Roman empire, with a promise of betraying every thing into his hands. This was accordingly done, and Rome captured.

But Genseric, barbarian-like and fickle, did not maintain his fidelity even to her; but, after firing the city and making an indiscriminate pillage, he retired, taking with him Eudoxia and her two daughters, and returned to Africa. The elder daughter, Eudocia, he espouses to his own son, Huneric; but the younger, Placidia, subsequently sends, together with her mother Eudoxia, with a royal escort to Byzantium, with the view of pacifying Marcian, who was exasperated both by the burning of Rome and the outrage upon the royal ladies. Placidia, in obedience to Marcian, consents to marry Olybrius, a distinguished member of the senate, who had come to Constantinople on the capture of Rome.

After Maximus, Avitus was emperor of the Romans for eight months; and on his decease by starvation, Majorian for more than a year: and after he had been treacherously murdered by Ricimer, master of the Roman armies, Severus for three years.

CHAPTER VIII

DEATH OF THE EMPEROR MARCIAN. MURDER OF PROTERIUS, BISHOP OF ALEXANDRIA. ELECTION OF TIMOTHY, SURNAMED ÆLURUS (THE CAT).

During the reign of Severus at Rome, Marcian exchanges his earthly sovereignty by a removal to a happier state, having reigned only seven years, but leaving behind him a truly royal monument in the memories of mankind. On learning this

AD 457

event, the people of Alexandria renewed their feud against Proterius with still greater exasperation and excessive heat: for the populace in general are an inflammable material, and allow very trivial pretexts to foment the flame of commotion, and not in the least degree that of Alexandria, which presumes on its numbers, chiefly an obscure and promiscuous rabble, and vaunts forth its impulses with excessive audacity. Accordingly, it is said that every one who is so disposed may, by employing any casual circumstance as a means of excitement, inspire the city with a frenzy of sedition, and hurry the populace in whatever direction and against whomsoever he chooses. Their general humor, however, is even of a sportive kind, as Herodotus records to have been the case with Amasis. Such, then, is the character of this people; who were, however, in all other respects by no means contemptible.

The people of Alexandria, accordingly, taking advantage of the prolonged absence of Dionysius, commander of the legions, in Upper Egypt, decree the elevation to the highest priestly grade, of Timotheus, surnamed Ælurus, who had formerly followed the monastic life, but had subsequently been admitted among the presbyters of the church of Alexandria; and, conducting him to the great church, styled that of Cæsar, elect him their bishop, though Proterius was still alive and discharged the functions of his office. There were present at the election, Eusebius, president of the church of Pelusium, and Peter the Iberian, bishop of the town of Majumas, according to the account given of the transaction by the writer of the life of Peter, who also says that Proterius was not killed by the populace, but by one of the soldiers. When Dionysius, on account of the urgency of these disorders, had occupied the city with the utmost dispatch, and was taking prompt measures to quench the towering conflagration of the sedition, some of the Alexandrians, at the instigation of Timotheus, according to the written report made to Leo, dispatch Proterius when he appeared, by thrusting a sword through his bowels, after he had fled for refuge to the holy baptistery. Suspending the body by a cord, they displayed it to the public in the quarter called Tetrapylum, jeering and vociferating that the victim was Proterius; and, after dragging it through the whole city, committed it to the flames; not even refraining themselves from tasting his intestines, like beasts of prey, according to the account of the entire transaction contained in the petition addressed by the Egyptian bishops and the whole clergy of Alexandria to Leo, who, as has been said, was invested with the imperial power on the death of Marcian. It was couched in the following terms:

"To the pious, Christ-loving, and divinely-appointed, the victorious and triumphant Augustus Leo, the petition of all the bishops of your Egyptian diocese, and the clergy of your most dignified and holy church of Alexandria. Having been granted, by divine grace, a boon to mankind, as such you cease not to exercise, next to God, a daily providence of the common weal, Augustus, most sacred of all emperors."

After some other matters, the petition proceeds: "And while undisturbed peace was prevailing among the orthodox people of our country and Alexandria, Timotheus, immediately after the holy synod at Chalcedon, being at that time a presbyter, severed himself from the Catholic church and faith, together with only four or five bishops and a few monks, of those who, as well as himself, were infected with the heretical errors of Apollinaris and his followers; on account of which opinions they were then deposed by Proterius, of divine memory, and the general synod of Egypt, and duly experienced the motion of the imperial will, in the sentence of banishment."

And afterwards it proceeds: "And having watched the opportunity afforded by the departure from this world to God of the emperor Marcian, of sacred memory, assuming then in blasphemous terms a bold tone of independence, and shamelessly anathematizing the holy and general synod at Chalcedon, while he drew after him a mercenary and disorderly multitude, and assailed the divine canons and ecclesiastical order, the commonwealth and the laws, he intruded himself upon the holy church of God, which at that time was possessed of a pastor and teacher in the person of our most holy father and archbishop, Proterius, duly performing the ordinary rites, and offering up to Christ, the Savior of us all, supplications in behalf of your pious sovereignty and your Christ-loving court."

And presently it proceeds: "And after the interval of only one day, while Proterius, beloved of God, was occupying, as usual, the episcopal residence, Timotheus, taking with him the two bishops who had been justly deposed, and the clergy who, as we have said, were condemned to banishment with them, as if he had received rightful ordination at the hands of the two, though not one of the orthodox bishops of the whole Egyptian diocese was present, as is customary on occasion of the ordinations of the bishop of the church of Alexandria—he possesses himself, as he presumed, of the archiepiscopal see, though manifestly guilty of an adulterous outrage on the church, as already having her rightful spouse in one who was performing the divine offices in her, and canonically occupied his proper throne."

And further on: "The blessed man could do nothing else than give place to wrath, according to what is written, and take refuge in the venerable baptistery from the assault of those who were pursuing him to death, a place which especially inspires awe even into barbarians and savages, though ignorant of its dignity, and the grace which flows from it. Notwithstanding, however, those who were eager to carry into execution the design which Timotheus had from the first conceived, and who could not endure that his life should be protected by those undefiled precincts, neither reverenced the dignity of the place, nor yet the season (for it was the solemnity of the saving paschal feast), nor were awe-struck at the priestly office which mediates between God and man; but put the blameless man to death, cruelly butchering him with six others. They then drew forth his body, covered with wounds, and having dragged it in horrid procession with unfeeling mockery through almost every part of the city, ruthlessly loaded the senseless corpse with indignity, so far as to tear it limb from limb, and not even abstain from tasting, like beasts of prey, the flesh of him whom but just before they were supposed to have as a mediator between God and man. They then committed what remained of the body to the flames, and scattered the ashes to the winds, exceeding the utmost ferocity of wild beasts. Of all these transactions Timotheus was the guilty cause, and the skilful builder of the scheme of mischief."

Zacharias, however, while treating at length of these events, is of opinion that the greater part of the circumstances thus detailed actually occurred, but through the fault of Proterius, by his instigation of serious disturbances in the city, and that these outrages were committed, not by the populace, but by some of the soldiery; grounding his opinion on a letter addressed by Timotheus to Leo. In consequence, however, of these proceedings, Stilas is sent out by the emperor to chastise them.

CHAPTER IX

LETTER FROM THE EMPEROR LEO.

Leo also addresses circular letters of inquiry to the bishops throughout the empire and the most distinguished monastics, relating to the synod at Chalcedon and the ordination of Timotheus, surnamed Ælurus, accompanying them with copies of the petitions which had been presented to him on the part both of Proterius and Timotheus. The circular letters were couched in the following terms:

A copy of the sacred epistle of the most pious emperor Leo to Anatolius, bishop of Constantinople, to the metropolitans throughout the whole world, and the other bishops.

"The emperor Cæsar Leo, pious, victorious, triumphant, supreme, ever-worshipful Augustus, to the bishop Anatolius. It has ever been a subject of prayer to my piety, that all the orthodox and most holy churches, and, indeed, the cities throughout the Roman dominion, should enjoy perfect tranquillity, and that nothing should befall them to disturb their settled serenity. The events, however, which have lately happened at Alexandria, we are assured, are known to your holiness: but that you may be more fully informed respecting the entire transaction, and the cause of so much tumult and confusion, we have forwarded to your sanctity copies of the petitions which the most reverent bishops and clergy of the before-mentioned city, and of the Egyptian diocese, presented to our piety against Timotheus, at the imperial city of Constantine; and, in addition, copies of the petitions presented to our serenity, at our sacred court, by persons from Alexandria on behalf of Timotheus; so that your holiness will be able distinctly to learn what have been the proceedings of the before-mentioned Timotheus, whom the people of Alexandria and their dignitaries, senators, and ship-masters request for their bishop, and what relates to the other transactions, as intimated by the tenor of the petitions, as well as regarding the synod at Chalcedon, to which these parties by no means assent, according as the matters are set forth by the petitions appended.

Your reverence will accordingly forthwith cause to assemble to you all the orthodox holy bishops who are now resident in the imperial city, as also the most reverent clergy; and, after carefully investigating and testing every circumstance, considering that Alexandria is at present disturbed, and that we are most solicitous for its settlement and tranquillity, declare your opinion respecting the before-mentioned Timotheus and the synod at Chalcedon, without any fear of man, and apart from all favor or dislike; setting before your eyes only the fear of the Almighty, inasmuch as ye know that ye shall give account of this matter to His pure Godhead. This we enjoin, in order that, being perfectly informed by your letters, we may be able to frame the fitting issue on the entire matter."

The emperor wrote also in similar terms to the other bishops, and, as I have said, to the most distinguished among those who at that period were practicing the endurance of the bare and immaterial mode of life. Among these was Simeon, who first conceived the station on the pillar, and of whom I have made mention in the former part of the history; as well as Baradatus and Jacob, the Syrians.

CHAPTER X
REPLIES OF THE BISHOPS. AND OF SIMEON.

Accordingly, in the first instance, Leo, bishop of the elder Rome, both wrote in defense of the synod at Chalcedon, and declared the ordination of Timotheus to be null, as having been irregularly performed. This epistle the emperor Leo dispatches to Timotheus, president of the church of Alexandria; Diomedes, the silentiary, executing the imperial commission: and Timotheus wrote in rejoinder, excepting to the synod at Chalcedon and the epistle of Leo. Of these documents copies are preserved in the collection called the Circulars: but I have omitted them, to avoid encumbering the matter on hand with too great a number.

The bishops, too, of the other cities, expressed their adherence to the determinations framed at Chalcedon, and unanimously condemned the ordination of Timotheus. Amphilochius alone, bishop of Side, wrote an epistle, loudly reprobating the ordination of Timotheus, but also rejecting the synod at Chalcedon. Zacharias the rhetorician has also treated of these transactions, and has inserted the epistle itself of Amphilochius in his work. Simeon, too, of holy memory, wrote two epistles on the occasion; namely, to the emperor Leo, and to Basilius, bishop of Antioch. The latter, as being brief, I insert in this my history, as follows:

"To my lord, the most religious and holy servant of God, the archbishop Basilius, the sinful and humble Simeon wishes health in the Lord. Well may we now say, my lord: Blessed be God, who has not rejected our prayer, nor withdrawn his mercy from us sinners. For, on the receipt of the letters of your worthiness, I admired the zeal and piety of our sovereign, beloved of God, which he manifested and still manifests toward the holy fathers and their unshaken faith. And this gift is not from ourselves, as says the holy apostle, but from God, who, through your prayers, bestowed on him this readiness of mind."

And presently he proceeds: "On this account, I also, though mean and worthless, the refuse of the monks, have conveyed to his majesty my judgement respecting the creed of the six hundred and thirty holy fathers assembled at Chalcedon, firmly resolving to abide by the faith then revealed by the Holy Spirit: for if, in the midst of two or three who are gathered in His name, the Savior is present, how could it be otherwise, than that the Holy Spirit should be throughout in the midst of so many and so distinguished holy fathers?"

And afterwards he proceeds: "Wherefore be stout and courageous in the cause of true piety, as was also Joshua the son of Nun, the servant of the Lord, in behalf of the children of Israel. I beg you to salute from me all the reverent clergy who are under your holiness, and the blessed and most faithful laity."

CHAPTER XI

PUNISHMENT OF TIMOTHY.

On these grounds Timotheus is sentenced to banishment, and Gangra is in his case also named as the place of exile.

The Alexandrians then elect another Timotheus, variously surnamed Basilicus and Salofacialus. Anatolius dies, and Gennadius succeeds him in the see of the imperial city. His successor is Acacius, who had been master of the Orphan Hospital in that city.

CHAPTER XII

EARTHQUAKE AT ANTIOCH.

During the second year of the reign of Leo, an extraordinary shock and concussion of the earth took place at Antioch, preceded by certain excesses of the populace, which reached the extreme of frenzy, and surpassed the ferocity of beasts, forming, as it were, a prelude to such a calamity. This grievous visitation occurred in the five hundred and sixth year of the free prerogatives of the city, about the fourth hour of the night, on the fourteenth day of the month Gorpiæus, which the Romans call September, on the eve of the Lord's day, in the eleventh cycle of the indiction; and was the sixth on record after a lapse of three hundred and forty-seven years, since the earthquake under Trajan; for that occurred when the city was in the hundred and fifty-ninth year of its independence; but this, which happened in the time of Leo, in the five hundred and sixth, according to the most diligent authorities.

This earthquake threw down nearly all the houses of the New City, which was very populous, and contained not a single vacant or altogether unoccupied spot, but had been highly embellished by the rival liberality of the emperors. Of the structures composing the palace, the first and second were thrown down: the rest, however, remained standing, together with the adjoining baths, which, having been previously useless, were now rendered serviceable to the necessities of the city, arising from the damage of the others. It also levelled the porticoes in front of the palace and the adjacent Tetrapylum, as well as the towers of the Hippodrome, which flanked the entrances, and some of the porticoes adjoining them. In the Old City, the porticoes and dwellings entirely escaped the overthrow; but it shattered a small portion of the baths of Trajan, Severus, and Hadrian, and also laid in ruins some parts of the quarter of houses named Ostracine, together with the porticoes, and levelled what was called the Nymphæum.

All these circumstances have been minutely detailed by John the rhetorician.[1] He says, that a thousand talents of gold were remitted to the city from the tributes by the emperor; and, besides, to individual citizens, the imposts of the houses destroyed: and that he also took measures for the restoration both of them and of the public buildings.

CHAPTER XIII

CONFLAGRATION AT CONSTANTINOPLE.

A similar, or even more terrible calamity, befell Constantinople, which took its rise from the quarter of the city bordering on the sea, and named Bosporium. The account is, that about dusk-hour, a demon of destruction in the form of a woman, or in reality a poor woman incited by a demon, for the story is told in both ways, carried a light into the market for the purpose of buying pickled victuals, and then having set down the light, stole away. Catching some tow, it raised a great flame, and in a moment set the apartment on fire. The conflagration, thus begun, soon consumed every thing within its reach, and afterwards continuing to spread for four days, not only over the more combustible materials, but buildings of stone, notwithstanding every effort to check it, at last destroyed the whole heart of the city from north to south, a space of five stadia in width, and fourteen in length; throughout which it left no building standing, either public or private, nor pillars nor arches of stone; but the hardest substances were as completely consumed as if they had been

AD 462

60

combustible. The ruin, at its northern extremity, which is where the docks are situated, extended from the Bosporium to the old temple of Apollo; at the southern, from the harbor of Julian as far as the houses near the oratory of the church of Unanimity; and in the center of the city, from the forum of Constantine to the Forum Tauri, as it is called: a pitiable and loathsome spectacle; for all the most conspicuous ornaments of the city, and whatever had been embellished with unrivalled magnificence, or adapted to public or private utility, had been swept together into huge heaps and impassable mounds, formed of various substances, whose former features were now so blended in one confused mass, that not even those who lived on the spot could recognize the different portions, and the place to which each had belonged.

CHAPTER XIV
OTHER PUBLIC CALAMITIES.

About the same time, when the Scythian war was gathering against the Eastern Romans, an earthquake visited Thrace, the Hellespont, Ionia, and the islands called Cyclades; so severe as to cause a universal overthrow in Cnidus and Cos. Priscus also records the occurrence of excessive rains about Constantinople and Bithynia, which descended like torrents for three or four days; when hills were swept down to the plains, and villages carried away by the deluge: islands also were formed in the lake Boane, not far from Nicomedia, by the masses of rubbish brought down by the waters. This evil, however, was subsequent to the former.

CHAPTER XV
MARRIAGE OF ZENO AND ARIADNE.

Leo bestows his daughter Ariadne on Zeno, who from his infancy had been called Aricmesius, but on his marriage

61

assumed the former name, derived from an individual who had attained great distinction among the Isaurians. The origin of the advancement of this Zeno, and the reason why he was preferred by Leo before all others, have been set forth by Eustathius the Syrian.

CHAPTER XVI

REIGN OF ANTHEMIUS. OF OLYBRIUS.
AND OTHER WESTERN PRINCES.

In compliance with an embassy from the Western Romans, Anthemius is sent out as emperor of Rome; to whom the late emperor Marcian had betrothed his own daughter. Basiliscus, brother to the emperor's wife Verina, is also sent out against Genseric, in command of a body of chosen troops: which transactions have been treated of with great exactness by Priscus the rhetorician; and how Leo, in repayment, as it were, for his own advancement, treacherously procures the death of Aspar, who had been the means of investing him with the sovereignty, and also of his sons, Ardaburius and Patricius; on the latter of whom he had previously bestowed the title of Cæsar, in order to conciliate Aspar. After the slaughter of Anthemius, in the fifth year of his reign, Olybrius is declared emperor by Ricimer; and after him appointment is made of Glycerius. Nepos possesses himself of the supreme power for five years, by the expulsion of Glycerius, whom he appoints to the bishopric of Salona, a city of Dalmatia. He is himself driven from power by Orestes, as was subsequently Romulus, surnamed Augustulus, the son of the latter, who was the last emperor of Rome, at an interval of thirteen hundred and three years from the reign of Romulus. Odoacer next sways the affairs of the Romans, declining the imperial title, but assuming that of king.

AD 476-493

CHAPTER XVII

DEATH OF THE EMPEROR LEO.

About the same time the emperor Leo, at Byzantium, departs his sovereignty, after having swayed it for seventeen years, and appointed to the empire Leo, the infant son of his daughter Ariadne and Zeno. Zeno then assumes the purple, being aided by the favor of Verina, the wife of Leo, towards her son-in-law. On the death of the child, which shortly followed, Zeno continued in sole possession of the sovereignty. The transactions which originated with him, or were directed against him, and whatever else befell him, the sequel shall detail, with the aid of the Superior Power.

AD 474

The proceedings of the synod at Chalcedon are here given in a compendious form.

CHAPTER XVIII

EPITOME OF THE ACTS OF THE COUNCIL OF CHALCEDON. *AD 451*

Paschasinus and Lucentius, bishops, and Boniface, a presbyter, filled the place of Leo, archpriest of the elder Rome; there being present Anatolius president of the church of Constantinople, Dioscorus bishop of Alexandria, Maximus of Antioch, and Juvenalis of Jerusalem, and with them their associate bishops; on whom attended also those who held the highest rank in the most excellent senate. To the latter the representatives of Leo alleged, that Dioscorus ought not to be seated with themselves, for such were their instructions from Leo; and that if this should be allowed, they would retire from the church. In reply to the question of the senators, what were the charges against Dioscorus, they stated, that he ought himself to render an account of his own decision, since he had unduly assumed the character of a judge, without being authorized by the bishop of Rome.

After this statement had been made, and Dioscorus stood in the midst, according to a decision of the senate, Eusebius, Bishop of Dorylæum, demanded, in the following words, that the petition should be read which he had presented to the sovereign power: "I have been wronged by Dioscorus; the faith has been wronged; Flavian the bishop was murdered, and together with myself unjustly deposed by him. Give directions that my petition be read."

On its being so ruled, the petition was read, couched in the following terms: "The petition of Eusebius, the very humble bishop of Dorylæum, in behalf of himself and the sainted Flavian, formerly bishop of Constantinople. It is the aim of your majesty to exercise a providential care of all your subjects, and stretch forth a protecting hand to all who are suffering wrong, and to those especially who are invested with the priesthood; for by this means service is rendered to God, from whom you have received the bestowal of supremacy and power over all regions under the sun. Inasmuch, then, as the Christian faith and we have suffered many outrages at the hands of Dioscorus, the most reverent bishop of the great city of the Alexandrians, we address ourselves to your piety in pursuance of our rights. The circumstances of the case are as follow:

"At the synod lately held at the metropolitan city of the Ephesians—would that it had never met, nor the world been thereby filled with mischiefs and tumult—the excellent Dioscorus, regarding neither the principle of justice nor the fear of God, sharing also in the opinions and feelings of the visionary and heretical Eutyches, though unsuspected by the multitude of being such as he afterwards showed himself, took occasion of the charge advanced by me against his fellow in doctrine, Eutyches, and the decision given by the sainted bishop Flavian, and having gathered a disorderly rabble, and procured an overbearing influence by bribes, made havoc as far as lay in his power, of the pious religion of the orthodox, and established the erroneous doctrine of Eutyches the monk, which had from the first been repudiated by the holy fathers.

Since, then, his aggressions against the Christian faith and us are of no trifling magnitude, we beseech and supplicate your majesty to issue, your commands to the same most reverent bishop Dioscorus, to defend himself against our allegations; namely, when the record of the acts which Dioscorus procured against us, shall be read before the holy synod; on the ground of which we are able to show, that he is estranged from the orthodox faith, that he strengthened a heresy utterly impious, that he wrongfully deposed and has cruelly outraged us. And this we will do on the issuing of your divine and revered mandates to the holy and universal synod of the bishops, highly beloved of God, to the effect that they should give a formal hearing to the matters which concern both us and the before-mentioned Dioscorus, and refer all the transactions to the decision of your piety, as shall seem fit to your immortal supremacy. If we obtain this our request, we shall ever pray for your everlasting rule, most divine sovereigns."

At the joint request of Dioscorus and Eusebius, the transactions of the second synod of Ephesus were publicly read; from which it appeared that the epistle of Leo had not obtained a reading, and that, too, when mention of the subject had been twice started. Dioscorus, being called upon to state the reason of this, said expressly that he had twice proposed that it should be done; and he then required that Juvenalis, bishop of Jerusalem, and Thalassius, bishop of Cæsarea, metropolis of Cappadocia Prima, should explain the circumstances, since they shared the presidency with himself. Juvenalis accordingly said that the reading of a sacred rescript, having precedency, had, at his decision, been interposed, and that no one had subsequently mentioned the epistle. Thalassius said that he had not opposed the reading, nor had he sufficient authority to enable him singly to signify that it should proceed.

The reading of the transactions was then proceeded with; and on some of the bishops excepting to certain passages as forgeries, Stephen, bishop of Ephesus, being asked which of his notaries were copyists in this place, named Julian, afterwards bishop of Lebedus, and Crispinus; but said that the notaries of Dioscorus would not allow them to act, but seized their fingers, so that they were in danger of most grievous treatment. He also affirmed, that on one and the same day he subscribed to the deposition of Flavian. To this statement, Acacius, bishop of Ariarathia, added, that they had all subscribed a blank paper by force and compulsion, being beset with innumerable evils, and surrounded by soldiers with deadly weapons.

Again, on the reading of another expression, Theodore, bishop of Claudiopolis, said that no one had uttered the words. And as the reading was thus proceeding, on the occurrence of a passage to the effect that Eutyches expressed his disapproval of those who affirmed that the flesh of our God and Lord and Savior Jesus Christ had descended from heaven, the acts testify that Eusebius, upon this, asserted that Eutyches had discarded indeed the term "from heaven," but had not proceeded to say from whence; and that Diogenes, bishop of Cyzicus, then urged him with the demand, "Tell us from whence;" but that further than this they were not allowed to press the question.

The acts then show: that Basil, bishop of Seleucia in Isauria, said, "I worship our one Lord Jesus Christ, the Son of God, the only Divine Word manifested after the incarnation and union in two natures;"—that the Egyptians clamored against this, "Let no one part the indivisible One; it is not proper to call the one Son two;" and that the Orientals exclaimed, "Anathema to him that parts! Anathema to him that divides!"—that Eutyches was asked, whether he affirmed two natures in Christ; to which he replied, that he held Christ to have been from two natures, before the union, but that after the union there was only one;—that Basil said, that unless he maintained two natures without severance and without confusion after the union, he maintained a confusion and commixture; but, notwithstanding, if he would add the terms "incarnate," and "invested with humanity," and should understand the incarnation and the assumption of humanity in the same sense as Cyril, he affirmed the same thing as themselves; for the Godhead derived from the Father was one thing, and humanity from His mother was another.

On the parties being asked why they had subscribed the deposition of Flavian, the acts show that the Orientals exclaimed, "We have all erred; we all entreat pardon." Again, as the reading proceeded, they show that the bishops were asked why, when Eusebius wished to enter the council, they did not allow him. To this Dioscorus replied, that Elpidius presented a commonitorium, and solemnly affirmed that the emperor Theodosius had given command that Eusebius should not be admitted. The acts show that Juvenalis also gave the same answer. Thalassius however, said that authority in the matter did not rest with himself. These replies were disallowed by the magistrates, on the ground that, such excuses were insufficient when the faith was at issue: upon which Dioscorus recriminated; "In what respect does the presence of Theodoret at this time accord with the observance of the canons?" The senators rejoined, that Theodoret had been admitted in the character of an accuser; but Dioscorus signified, that he was sitting in the position of a bishop. The senators again said, that Eusebius and Theodoret occupied the position of accusers, as Dioscorus himself that of an accused person.

The entire transactions of the second synod at Ephesus having been accordingly read, and, in like manner, the sentence against Flavian and Eusebius, as far as the place where Hilary had declared a protest, the Oriental bishops and their party exclaimed, "Anathema to Dioscorus: Christ has at this moment deposed Dioscorus. Flavian was deposed by Dioscorus. Holy Lord, do thou avenge him! Orthodox sovereign, do thou avenge him! Many be the years of Leo! Many be the years of the patriarch!"

When the sequel of the document had been read, showing that all the assembled bishops had assented to the deposition of Flavian, the most illustrious magistrates ruled as follows: "Concerning the orthodox and catholic faith, we are clearly of opinion that a more accurate investigation should be made in a more complete assemblage of the synod tomorrow. But since it appears that Flavian, of pious memory, and Eusebius, the most reverent bishop of Dorylæum, were not in error concerning the faith, but were unjustly deposed, both from the examination of the acts and decrees, and from the present confession of those who presided in the synod, that themselves were in error, and the deposition was null; it seems to us, according to the good pleasure of God, to be just, with the approval of our most divine and pious lord, that Dioscorus, the most reverent bishop of Alexandria; Juvenalis, the most reverent bishop of Jerusalem; Thalassius, the most reverent bishop of Cæsarea; Eusebius, the most, reverent bishop of Ancyra; Eustathius, the most reverent bishop of Berytus; and Basil, the most reverent bishop of Seleucia, in Isauria, should be subjected to the same penalty, by being deprived, through this holy synod, in accordance with the canons, of the episcopal dignity; with a reference of whatever is consequent, to the imperial supremacy."

On this the Orientals exclaimed, "This is a just decision;" and the Illyrian bishops, "We were all in error; let us all be deemed deserving of pardon." When the Orientals had again exclaimed, "This is a just verdict: Christ has deposed the murderer: Christ has avenged the martyrs!" the senators ruled to the effect, that each of the assembled bishops should severally put forth his own formulary of faith, under the assurance that the belief of the most divine emperor was in accordance with the exposition of the three hundred fathers at Nicæa, and of the hundred and fifty at Constantinople; and with the epistles of the holy fathers, Gregory, Basil, Hilary, Athanasius, and Ambrose, as well as the two of Cyril, which were made public in the first synod at Ephesus; inasmuch as upon these grounds Leo, the most reverent bishop of the Elder Rome, had deposed Eutyches. In this manner was closed the present meeting of the council.

At the next, composed of the most holy bishops alone, Eusebius presented libels in behalf of himself and Flavian, in which he objected to Dioscorus, that he held the same opinions as Eutyches, and had deprived themselves of the priesthood. He further charged him with inserting in the transactions expressions which were not uttered in the synod, and having procured their subscription to a blank paper. He petitioned that the entire acts of the second synod at Ephesus should be annulled by vote of those who were now assembled; that themselves should retain their priesthood; and that foul tenet be anathematized.

After the reading of this document, he also required that his adversary should be present. When this had been ruled in the affirmative, Aetius, archdeacon and primicerius of the notaries, stated that he had proceeded to Dioscorus, as also to the others; but that he said he was not permitted by the persons on guard to appear. It was then decided that Dioscorus should be sought in front of the place of meeting; and, on his not being found, Anatolius, bishop of Constantinople, ruled that he ought to be summoned, and be present before the synod. This course having been adopted, the delegates, on their return, said that he had replied: "I am under restraint. Let these say whether they leave me free to proceed thither;" and to their intimation that they were deputed to himself, and not to the civil powers, his answer was stated to be: "I am ready to proceed to the holy and universal synod, but I am prevented." To this statement Himerius added, that the Assistant of the Master of the Sacred Offices had met them on their return, in company with whom the bishops had again visited Dioscorus and that he had taken some notes of what then passed. These were then read, and set forth the precise words of Dioscorus, as follows:

"Upon calm reflection, and due consideration of my interest, I thus reply. Whereas, at the former meeting of the synod, the most illustrious magistrates ruled upon many several points, and I am now summoned to a second, having for its object a modification of the preceding matters; I pray that the most illustrious magistrates who attended on the former occasion, and the sacred senate, should do so on the present also, in order that the same points may be again debated."

The acts show that Acacius then replied in the following words: "The great and holy synod, in requiring the presence of your holiness, has not in view a modification of what was transacted in the presence of the most illustrious magistrates and the sacred senate but it has deputed us merely that you should have a place in the meeting, and that your holiness should not be wanting to it."

Dioscorus replied, according to the acts, "You have just told me that Eusebius had presented libels. I pray that the matters touching myself may be again sifted in the presence of the magistrates and the senate."

Then follow other similar matters. Afterwards persons were again sent with a commission to urge Dioscorus to appear; who, on their return, said that they had taken notes of his words. From these it appears that he said: " I have already signified to your piety, both that I am suffering from sickness and that I demand that the most illustrious magistrates and the sacred senate should also on the present occasion attend the investigation of the matters at issue. Since, however, my sickness has increased, on this ground I am withholding my attendance."

Cecropius, then, as appears from the acts, intimated to Dioscorus, that but a short time before he had made no mention of sickness, and, accordingly, he ought to satisfy the requisitions of the canons. To whom Dioscorus rejoined: "I have said once for all, that the magistrates ought to be present." Then Rufinus, bishop of Samosata, told him that the matters mooted were under canonical regulation, and that on his appearance he would be at liberty to make whatever statements he chose. To the enquiry of Dioscorus, whether Juvenalis, Thalassius, and Eustathius were present, he replied that this was nothing to the purpose. The acts show that Dioscorus said in answer, that he prayed the Christ-loving emperor to the effect that the magistrates should be present, and also those who had acted as judges in conjunction with himself. To this the deputies rejoined that Eusebius accused him only, and there was accordingly no occasion that all should be present. Dioscorus replied, that the others who had acted with him ought to be present, for the suit of Eusebius did not affect himself individually, but rested in fact upon a judgment in which they had all united. When the deputies still insisted upon this point, Dioscorus summarily replied:" What I have said, I have said once for all; and I have now nothing further to say."

Upon this report, Eusebius stated that his charge was against Dioscorus only, and against no other person; and he required that he should be summoned a third time. Aetius then, in continuance, informed them that certain persons from Alexandria, professing to be clerks, together with several laymen, had lately presented libels against Dioscorus, and, standing outside, were now invoking the synod. When, accordingly, in the first place Theodorus, a deacon of the holy church at Alexandria, had presented libels and afterwards Ischyrion, a deacon, Athanasius, a presbyter, and nephew of Cyril, and also Sophronius in which they charged Dioscorus with blasphemies offenses against the person, and violent

71

seizures of money; a third summons was issued urging him to attend.

Those who were accordingly selected for this service, on their return, reported Dioscorus to have said: "I have already sufficiently informed your piety on this point, and cannot add any thing further."

Since Dioscorus had persisted in the same reply, while the delegates continued to press him, the bishop Paschasinus said: "At length, after being summoned a third time, Dioscorus has not appeared:" and he then asked what treatment he deserved. To this, when the bishops had replied that he had rendered himself obnoxious to the canons, and Proterius, bishop of Smyrna, had observed, that when Flavian had been murdered, no suitable measures had been taken with respect to him; the representatives of Leo, bishop of the elder Rome, made a declaration as follows:

"The aggressions committed by Dioscorus, lately bishop of the great city Alexandria, in violation of canonical order and the constitution of the church, have been clearly proved by the investigations at the former meeting, and the proceedings of today. For, not to mention the mass of his offenses, he did, on his own authority, uncanonically admit to communion his partisan Eutyches, after having been canonically deprived by his own bishop, namely, our sainted father and archbishop Flavian; and this before he sat in council with the other bishops at Ephesus. To them, indeed, the holy see granted pardon for the transactions of which they were not the deliberate authors, and they have hitherto continued obedient to the most holy archbishop Leo, and the body of the holy and universal synod; on which account he also admitted them into communion with him, as being his fellows in faith. Whereas Dioscorus has continued to maintain a haughty carriage, on account of those very circumstances over which he ought to have bewailed, and humbled himself to the earth. Moreover, he did not even allow the epistle to be read which the blessed pope Leo had addressed to Flavian, of holy memory; and that too, notwithstanding he was repeatedly exhorted thereto by the bearers, and had promised with an oath to that effect. The result of the epistle not being read, has been to fill the most holy churches throughout the world with scandals and mischief.

"Notwithstanding however, such presumption, it was our purpose to deal mercifully with him as regards his past impiety, as we had done with the other bishops, although they had not held an equal judicial authority with him. But inasmuch as he has, by his subsequent conduct, overshot his former iniquity, and has presumed to pronounce excommunication against Leo, the most holy and religious archbishop of great Rome; since, moreover, on the presentation of a paper full of grievous charges against him to the holy and great synod, he refused to appear, though once, twice, and thrice canonically summoned by the bishops, pricked no doubt by his own conscience; and since he has unlawfully given reception to those who had been duly deposed by different synods; he had thus, by variously trampling upon the laws of the church, given his own verdict against himself.

"Wherefore Leo, the most blessed and holy archbishop of the great and elder Rome, has, by the agency of ourselves and the present synod, in conjunction with the thrice-blessed and all honored Peter, who is the rock and basis of the Catholic church, and the foundation of the orthodox faith, deprived him of the episcopal dignity, and severed him from every priestly function. Accordingly, this holy and great synod decrees the provisions of the canons on the aforesaid Dioscorus."

After the ratification of this proceeding by Anatolius and Maximus, and by the other bishops, with exception of those who had been deposed together with Dioscorus by the senate, a relation of the matter was addressed to Marcian by the synod, and the instrument of deposition was transmitted to Dioscorus, to the following effect: "On account of contempt of the sacred canons, and thy contumacy regarding this holy and universal synod, inasmuch as, in addition to the other offenses of which thou hast been convicted, thou didst not appear, even when summoned the third time by this great and holy synod, according to the sacred canons, in order to reply to the charges made against thee; know then that thou hast been deposed from thy bishopric, on the thirteenth day of this present month, October, by the holy and universal synod, and deprived of all ecclesiastical rank." After a letter had been written to the bishops of the most holy church at Alexandria on this subject, and an edict had been framed against Dioscorus, the proceedings of this meeting were closed.

After the business of the preceding meeting had terminated in this manner, the members of the synod, again assembling, replied to the inquiry of the magistrates, who desired to be informed respecting the orthodox doctrine, that there was no need that any further formulary should be framed, now that the matter relating to Eutyches had been brought to a close and had received a conclusive determination at the hands of the Roman bishop, with the further accordance of all parties. After the bishops had with one voice exclaimed that they all held the same language, and the magistrates had ruled that each patriarch, selecting one or two persons of his own diocese, should come forward into the midst of the council in order to make a declaration of their several opinions; Florentius, bishop of Sardis, prayed a respite, so that they might approach the truth with due deliberation: and Cecropius, bishop of Sebastopolis, spoke as follows. "The faith has been well set forth by the three hundred and eighteen holy fathers, and has been confirmed by the holy fathers Athanasius, Cyril, Celestine, Hilary, Basil, Gregory, and again, on the present occasion, by the most holy Leo. We accordingly require that the words both of the three hundred and eighteen holy fathers and of the most holy Leo be now read."

At the conclusion of the reading the whole synod

exclaimed, "This is the faith of the orthodox; thus we all believe; thus does the Pope Leo believe; thus did Cyril believe; thus has the Pope expounded."

Another interlocution was then issued, that, the form set forth by the hundred and fifty fathers should also be read: which was accordingly done; and the members of the synod exclaimed, "This is the faith of all; this is the faith of the orthodox; thus do we all believe!"

Then Aetius, the archdeacon, said that he held in his hand the epistle of the divine Cyril to Nestorius which all who were assembled at Ephesus had ratified by their individual subscriptions; as also another epistle of the same Cyril addressed to John of Antioch, which had itself also been confirmed. These he earnestly prayed might be read. Agreeably with an interlocution on the point, both were then read; a portion of the former being precisely as follows:

"Cyril to our most reverent fellow minister Nestorius. Certain persons, as I am informed, treat my rebuke with levity in the presence of your holiness, and that, too, repeatedly, taking especial occasion for that purpose of the meetings of the authorities; perhaps also with the idea of gratifying your own ears."

Afterwards it proceeds. " The declaration, then, of the holy and great synod was this: that the only begotten Son, begotten naturally of God the Father, very God of very God, light of light, by whose agency the Father made all things, descended, was incarnate, assumed humanity, suffered, rose again on the third day, ascended into heaven. This declaration we, too, ought to follow, carefully considering what is signified by the expression, that the Divine Word was incarnate and assumed humanity. For we do not affirm that the nature of the Word by undergoing a change became flesh, nor yet was even converted into a complete human being, consisting of soul and body; but this we rather maintain, that the Word, by uniting personally with himself flesh, animated by a rational soul, became man in an ineffable and incomprehensible manner, and bore the title of the Son of Man, not in respect of mere will or pleasure, nor even, as it were, in an assumption of person merely; and, further, that the natures which conspired to the true unity, were different, but from both is one Christ and Son; not as though the difference of the natures had been done away for the sake of the union, but they had rather consummated for us the one Lord and Christ and Son, from both the Godhead and the manhood, by their ineffable and mysterious coalition for unity."

And presently the epistle proceeds. "But since, for our sakes and for our salvation, having personally united humanity with himself, he came forth from a woman; in this respect he is said also to have been born carnally. For he was not born in the first instance an ordinary man of the holy Virgin, and then the Word descended upon him: but the Word, having been united from the very womb, is said to have undergone a carnal nativity, as it were, by an assumption of the nativity of his own flesh. In this manner we say that He suffered and rose again; as though the Word of God had endured, as regards his own nature, stripes or piercings of nails, or the other wounds, for the Deity is impassible, as being incorporeal. Since, however, his own body underwent these circumstances, Himself is said, on the other hand, to have suffered them on our behalf, inasmuch as the impassible being was in the suffering body."

The greater part of the other epistle has been inserted in the preceding portion of this history. It contains, however, a passage to the following effect, which John, bishop of Antioch wrote, and Cyril entirely approved. "We confess the holy Virgin to be the Mother of God, because from her the Divine Word was incarnate and assumed humanity, and from the very conception united with himself the temple which was derived from her. With respect, however, to the evangelical and apostolical language concerning our Lord, we know that the expressions of the divinely inspired men are sometimes comprehensive, as in respect of a single person; sometimes distinctive, as in respect of two natures; and that they deliver such as are of divine import, in reference to the Godhead of Christ, and those which are humble, in reference to His manhood." Cyril then subjoins the following words: "On reading these your sacred expressions, we find that we ourselves hold the same opinion: for there is one Lord, one faith, one baptism. We accordingly glorify God, the Savior of all, rejoicing mutually, because both our churches and yours hold a faith which is in accordance with the inspired scriptures, and the tradition of our holy fathers."

After the reading of these epistles, the members of the synod exclaimed in these words: "Thus do we believe; thus does the Pope Leo believe. Anathema to him that divides and to him that confounds! This is the faith of Leo the archbishop. Thus does Leo believe. Thus do Leo and Anatolius believe. Thus do we all believe. As Cyril believed, so do we. Eternal be the memory of Cyril! Agreeably with the epistles of Cyril do we also think. Thus did we believe; thus do we now believe. Leo the archbishop thus thinks, thus believes, thus has written."

An interlocution having been given to that effect, the epistle of Leo was also read, in a translation, and is inserted in the acts; the bishops at its conclusion exclaiming, "This is the faith of the fathers: this is the faith of the Apostles. Thus do we all believe: thus do the orthodox believe. Anathema to him who does not thus believe! Peter has uttered these words through Leo. Thus have the Apostles taught. Leo has taught truly and piously: thus has Cyril taught. The teaching of Leo and Cyril is the same. Anathema to him who does not thus believe! This is the true faith. Thus do the orthodox think. This is the faith of the fathers. Why was not this read at Ephesus? This did Dioscorus withhold."

It is contained in the acts that when the bishops of Illyria and Palestine had expressed some hesitation, after the following passage of the epistle had been read: "In order to the discharge of the debt of our natural state, the divine nature was united to the passible, that one and the same person, the man Christ Jesus, being the mediator between God and man might be enabled from the one part to die, but incapable of decease from the other, such being the process adapted to our cure;" that upon this Aetius, archdeacon of the most holy church of Constantinople, produced a passage from Cyril to the following purport: "Since, however, His own body by the grace of God, as says the Apostle Paul, tasted death for every man, Himself is said to have suffered the death on our behalf; not that he experienced death to the extent of his own nature, for it would be madness to say or think this, but because, as I said before, his flesh tasted death."

Again, when the bishops of Illyria and Palestine had expressed their hesitation at the following passage of the epistle of Leo: "For there operates in each form its peculiar property, in union with what belongs to the other; the Word working that which pertains to the Word, and the body discharging that which pertains to the body; and the one shines forth by the miracles, the other was subjected to the insults;" upon this the said Aetius read a passage of Cyril as follows: "The rest of the expressions are especially appropriate to deity; others, again, are equally suited to manhood; and some hold, as it were, an intermediate place, presenting the Son of God as being God and man at the same time." Afterwards, when the same bishops hesitated at another part of the epistle of Leo, which is as follows: "Although in our Lord Jesus Christ there is altogether one person, of God and man, yet the one part from which was derived to the other a community of ignominy, is distinct from that from which proceeded a community of glory; for from us was derived the manhood, which is inferior to the Father, and from the Father the Godhead, which partakes equality with the Father;" Theodoret said to adjust the point, that the blessed Cyril had also expressed himself thus:

"That He both became man and at the same time did not lay aside His proper nature; for the latter continued as before, though dwelling in what was different from it; namely, the divine nature in conjunction with humanity." Afterwards, when the illustrious magistrates asked whether any one still hesitated, all replied that they no longer entertained any doubt.

Atticus, bishop of Nicopolis, then begged a respite of a few days, in order that a formulary might be framed of the matters which were approved by God and the holy fathers. He also prayed that they might have the epistle which was addressed by Cyril to Nestorius, in which he exhorts him to assent to his twelve chapters. All expressed their concurrence in these requests; and when the magistrates had ruled that a respite of five days should be allowed, in order to their assembling with Anatolius, president of Constantinople, all the bishops signified their approval saying, "Thus do we believe, thus do we all believe. Not one of us hesitates. We have all subscribed."

Upon this it was ruled as follows: "There is no necessity that you should all assemble; since, however, it is reasonable that the minds of those who have hesitated should be confirmed, let the most reverent bishop Anatolius select from among the subscribers whomsoever he may deem proper for the information of those who have doubted."

Upon this the members of the synod proceeded to exclaim, "We entreat for the fathers. The fathers to the synod. Those who accord with Leo to the synod. Our words to the emperor. Our prayers to the orthodox sovereign. Our prayers to Augusta. We have all erred. Let indulgence be granted to all."

Upon this, those who belonged to the church of Constantinople cried out, "But, few are exclaiming. The synod is not speaking."

Then the Orientals shouted, "The Egyptian to exile!"

And the Illyrians, "We entreat compassion upon all;" and again the Orientals, "The Egyptian to exile!"

While the Illyrians persisted in their prayer, the Constantinopolitan clergy shouted, "Dioscorus to exile! The Egyptian to exile! The heretic to exile!" and again the Illyrians and their party, "We have all erred. Grant indulgence to all. Dioscorus to the synod! Dioscorus to the churches!"

After further proceedings of the same kind, the business of this meeting was brought to a close.

At the next meeting, when the senators had ruled that the forms which had been already enacted should be read, Constantine, the secretary, read from a paper, as follows: "Concerning the orthodox and catholic faith, we are agreed that a more exact inquiry should take place before a fuller assembly of the council, at its next meeting. But inasmuch as it has been shown, from examination of the acts and decrees, and from the oral testimony of the presidents of that synod, who admit that themselves were in error, and the deposition was void, that Flavian, of pious memory, and the most reverent bishop Eusebius, were convicted of no error concerning the faith, and were wrongfully deposed, it seems to us, according to God's good pleasure, to be a just proceeding, if approved by our most divine and pious sovereign, that Dioscorus, the most reverent bishop of Alexandria; Juvenalis, the most reverent bishop of Jerusalem; Thalassius, the most reverent bishop of Cæsarea, in Cappadocia; Eusebius, the most reverent bishop of Ancyra; Eustathius, the most reverent bishop of Berytus; and Basilius, the most reverent bishop of Seleucia, in Isauria; who exercised sway and precedency in that, synod; should be subjected to the selfsame penalty, by suffering at the hands of the holy synod deprivation of their episcopal dignity, according to the canons; whatever is consequent hereupon, being submitted to the cognizance of the emperor's sacred supremacy."

After several other readings, the assembled bishops, being asked whether the letters of Leo accorded with the faith of the three hundred and eighteen holy fathers who met at Nicæa, and that of the hundred and fifty in the imperial city, Anatolius, president of Constantinople, and all who were present, replied, that the epistle of Leo accorded with the before-mentioned fathers; and he further subscribed the epistle. At this stage of the proceedings the members of the synod exclaimed: "We all concur: we all approve: we all believe alike: we all hold the same sentiments: thus do we all believe. The fathers to the synod! The subscribers to the synod! Many be the years of the emperor! Many be the years of Augusta! The fathers to the synod: those who agree with us in faith, to the synod! Many be the years of the emperor! Those who agree with us in opinion, to the synod! Many be the years of the emperor! We have all subscribed. As Leo thinks, so do we."

An interlocution was then pronounced to the following effect. "We have referred these matters to our most sacred and pious lord, and are now waiting the answer of his piety. But your reverence will give account to God concerning Dioscorus, who has been deposed by you without the knowledge of our most sacred sovereign and ourselves, and concerning the five for whom you are now making entreaty, and concerning all the acts of the synod."

They then expressed their approval, saying "God has deposed Dioscorus; Dioscorus has been justly deposed. Christ has deposed Dioscorus." Afterwards, on the presentation of a response from Marcian, leaving the case of those who had been deposed to the decision of the bishops, as the interlocution of the magistrates had set forth; they made entreaty in the following words. "We pray that they may be admitted: our fellows in doctrine, to the synod: our fellows in opinion, to the synod: the subscribers to the epistle of Leo, to the synod." They were accordingly, by an interlocution to that effect numbered with the members of the synod.

Then were read the petitions presented from the Egyptian diocese to the emperor Marcian; which in addition to other matters, contain the following: "We agree in opinion with what the three hundred and eighteen fathers at Nicæa, and the blessed Athanasius, and the sainted Cyril have set forth, anathematizing every heresy, both those of Arius, of Eunomius, of Manes, of Nestorius, and that of those who say, that the flesh of our Lord was derived from heaven and not from the holy Mother of God and ever virgin Mary, in like manner with ourselves, with the exception of sin."

Upon this, the whole synod exclaimed: "Why have they not anathematized the doctrine of Eutyches? Let them subscribe the epistle of Leo, anathematizing Eutyches and his doctrines. Let them concur with the epistle of Leo. They intend to jeer us, and be gone."

In reply, the bishops from Egypt stated, that the Egyptian bishops were numerous and that they themselves could not assume to represent those who were absent: and they prayed the synod to await their archbishop, that they might be guided by his judgment, as usage required: for if they should do anything before the appointment of their head, the whole diocese would assail them. After many entreaties on this subject, which were stoutly resisted by the synod, it was ruled, that a respite should be granted to the bishops from Egypt, until their archbishop should be ordained.

Then petitions were presented from certain monks; the purport of which was that they should not be compelled to subscribe certain papers, before the synod which the emperor had summoned should have assembled, and its determinations be made known. After these had been read, Diogenes, bishop of Cyzicus, stated that Barsumas, one of the persons present, had been the murderer of Flavian, for he had exclaimed "Slay him!" and, though not a party to the petition, had improperly obtained admission. Upon this all the bishops exclaimed: "Barsumas has desolated all Syria; he has let loose upon us a thousand monks."

After an interlocution, to the effect that the assembled

monks should await the determination of the synod, they demanded that the libels which they had drawn up should be read; one requisition therein contained being that Dioscorus and the bishops of his party should be present in the synod. In reply to which all the bishops exclaimed: "Anathema to Dioscorus! Christ has deposed Dioscorus! Cast out such persons. Away with outrage; away with violence from the synod! Our words to the emperor! Away with outrage; away with infamy from the synod!"

After a repetition of these exclamations, it was ruled that the remainder of the libels should be read: wherein it was affirmed, that the deposition of Dioscorus was improper; that, when a matter of faith was before the council, he ought to share in its deliberations, and that, if this were not granted, they would shake their garments from the communion of the assembled bishops. In reference to these expressions, Aetius, the archdeacon, read a canon against those who separate themselves. Again, when, at the questions of the most holy bishops, the monks manifested disagreement, and afterwards at an interrogation put by Aetius in the name of the synod, some anathematized Nestorius and Eutyches, while others declined; it was ruled by the magistrates, that the petitions of Faustus and the other monks should be read: which prayed the emperor no longer to sanction the monks who had lately opposed the orthodox doctrines. Whereupon Dorotheus, a monk, termed Eutyches orthodox: in reply to whom various doctrinal points were stated by the magistrates.

At the fifth meeting, the magistrates ruled that the determinations relating to the faith should be published; and Asclepiades, a deacon of Constantinople, read a formulary, which it was resolved should not be inserted in the acts. Some dissented from it, but the majority approved it: and on the utterance of counter exclamations, the magistrates said that Dioscorus affirmed that he had deposed Flavian on his asserting two natures, whereas the formulary contained the expression "from two natures." To this Anatolius replied, that Dioscorus had not been deposed on a point of faith, but because he had excommunicated Leo, and, after having been thrice summoned, did not appear. The magistrates then required that the substance of the epistle of Leo should be inserted in the formulary; but since the bishops objected, and maintained that no other formulary could be framed, inasmuch as a complete one already existed, a relation was made to the emperor; who commanded that six of the Oriental bishops, three from Pontus, three from Asia, three from Thrace, and three from Illyria, should, together with Anatolius and the vicars of Rome, assemble in the sanctuary of the martyr, and rightly frame the rule of faith, or put forth each his several declaration of faith; or be assured that the synod must be held in the West.

On this, being required to state whether they followed Dioscorus when affirming Christ was from two natures; or Leo, that there were two natures in Christ; they exclaimed that they agreed with Leo, and that those who contradicted, were Eutychians. The magistrates then said, that in accordance with the language of Leo, a clause should be added, to the effect that there were two natures united in Christ, without change, or severance or confusion; and they entered the sanctuary of the holy martyr Euphemia, in company with Anatolius and the vicars of Leo, as well as Maximus of Antioch, Juvenalis of Jerusalem, Thalassius of Cæsarea in Cappadocia, and others; and on their return, the formulary of faith was read, as follows. "Our Lord and Savior Jesus Christ," and so forth, as it has been inserted in a previous part of the history.

When all had exclaimed, "This is the faith of the fathers: let the metropolitans at once subscribe! This is the faith of the Apostles: by this are we all guided: thus do we all think!" the magistrates ruled, that the formulary, thus framed by the fathers and approved by all should be referred to the imperial supremacy.

At the sixth meeting Marcian was present, and harangued the bishops on the subject of unanimity. At the command of the emperor, the formulary was read by Aetius, archdeacon of Constantinople, and all subscribed it. The emperor then asked, whether the formulary had been composed with the approbation of all: upon which all declared their confirmation of it by expressions of approval. Again the emperor twice addressed them, and all applauded. At the emperor's suggestion certain canons were enacted, and metropolitan rank was conferred upon Chalcedon. The emperor further commanded the bishops to remain three or four days; that each one should move the synod on whatever matters he might choose in the presence of the magistrates; and such as were judged proper, should take effect. The meeting was then closed.

Another was held, at which canons were enacted; and at the next, Juvenalis and Maximus came to an agreement that Antioch should have for its province the two Phœnicias and Arabia; and Jerusalem, the three Palestines; which was ratified by an interlocution of the magistrates and bishops.

At the ninth meeting, the case of Theodoret was mooted. He anathematized Nestorius, saying, "Anathema to Nestorius, and to him who does not affirm the holy Virgin Mary to be Mother of God, and to him who divides into two Sons the one Son, the only begotten! I have also subscribed the formulary of faith and the epistle of Leo." Upon this he was restored to his see, by an interlocution of all parties.

At another meeting, the case of Ibas was discussed; and the judgment was read which had been passed upon him by Photius, bishop of Tyre, and Eustathius of Berytus; but the vote was deferred to the next meeting.

At the eleventh meeting, when the majority of the bishops had voted that Ibas should be restored to his episcopal rank, others, in rejoinder, said that his accusers were waiting outside, and required that they should be admitted. The proceedings in his case were then read; but when the magistrates ruled that the transactions at Ephesus respecting Ibas should also be read, the bishops replied that all the proceedings in the second synod at Ephesus were null, with the exception of the ordination of Maximus of Antioch. On this point, they further requested the emperor to decree that nothing should be valid which had been transacted at Ephesus subsequently to the first synod over which the sainted Cyril, president of Alexandria, had presided. It was judged right that Ibas should retain his bishopric.

At the next meeting, the case of Bassianus was inquired into, and it was judged fit that he should be removed and Stephen substituted: which measures were formally voted at the following meeting. At the thirteenth, the case was investigated of Eunomius of Nicomedia and Anastasius of Nicæa, who had a dispute about their respective cities. A fourteenth was also held, at which the case of Sabinianus was investigated. Finally, it was decided that the see of Constantinople should rank next after that of Rome.

NOTES

1.   John the rhetorician, more commonly known as John Malalas, was an Antiochene chronicler of the 6th century AD. The detailed account of the Antioch earthquake does not survive in the existing text (Whitby, p. 96, fn 137). See also the English translation of Malalas by Jeffreys, et al. (1986).

THE THIRD BOOK

CHAPTER I

CHARACTER OF THE EMPEROR ZENO.

Zeno on becoming, by the death of his son, sole emperor, as if entertaining an idea that his power was incomplete without an unrestrained pursuit of every pleasure that presented itself, so far abandoned himself from the first to the solicitations of desire, as to hesitate at nothing of all that is unseemly and illicit; but so thorough was his habitude in such things, that he esteemed it grovelling to practice them in concealment and privacy; but to do it openly, and as it were, in a conspicuous spot, truly royal and suited to none but an emperor: a notion base and servile; for the emperor is known, not by the circumstances of ordinary sway over others, but by those wherein he rules and sways himself, in guarding against the admission in his own person of whatever is indecorous; and being thus unconquered by loose indulgence, so as to be a living image of virtue for imitation and the instruction of his subjects. But he who lays himself open to the pleasures of sense, is unwittingly becoming a base slave, an unransomed captive, continually passing like worthless slaves, from the hands of one master to another; inasmuch as pleasures are an unnumbered train of mistresses, linked in endless succession; while the present enjoyment, so far from being lasting, is only the kindler and prelude to another, until a man either banishes the rabble rule of pleasures, becoming thus a sovereign instead of a victim of tyranny; or continuing a slave to the last, receives the portion of the infernal world.

CHAPTER II
INCURSIONS OF THE BARBARIANS.

In such a manner, then, had Zeno, from the commencement of his reign, depraved his course of life while, however, his subjects, both in the East and the West, were greatly distressed; in the one quarter, by the general devastations of the Scenite barbarians[1]; and in Thrace, by the inroads of the Huns, formerly known by the name of Massagetæ, who crossed the Ister without opposition: while Zeno himself, in barbarian fashion, was making violent seizure on whatever escaped them.

Arabs

CHAPTER III
INSURRECTION OF BASILISCUS. FLIGHT OF ZENO.

But on the insurrection of Basiliscus, the brother of Verina— for the disposition of his nearest connections was hostile, from the universal disgust at his most disgraceful life—he was utterly wanting in courage: for vice is craven and desponding, sufficiently indicating its unmanly spirit by submission to pleasures. Zeno fled with precipitation, and surrendered so great a sovereignty to Basiliscus without a struggle. He was also blockaded in his native district, Isauria, having with him his wife Ariadne, who had subsequently fled from her mother, and those parties who still continued loyal to him. Basiliscus, having thus acquired the Roman diadem, and bestowed on his son Marcus the title of Cæsar, adopted measures opposed to those of Zeno and his predecessors.

AD 475

CHAPTER IV
CIRCULAR OF BASILISCUS

At the instigation of an embassy of certain Alexandrians, Basiliscus summons Timotheus Ælurus from his exile, in the eighteenth year of his banishment; at which time Acacius held the episcopate of Constantinople. On his arrival at the imperial city, Timotheus persuades Basiliscus to address circular letters to the bishops in every quarter, and to anathematize the transactions at Chalcedon and the tome of Leo. They were to this effect.

THE CIRCULAR LETTER OF BASILISCUS

"The emperor Cæsar Basiliscus, pious, victorious, triumphant, supreme, ever-worshipful Augustus, and Marcus, the most illustrious Cæsar, to Timotheus, archbishop of the great city of the Alexandrians, most reverent and beloved of God. It has ever been our pleasure, that whatever laws have been decreed in behalf of the true and apostolic faith, by those our pious predecessors who have maintained the true service of the blessed and undecaying and life-giving Trinity, should never be inoperative; but we are rather disposed to enounce them as of our own enactment. We, preferring piety and zeal in the cause of our God and Savior Jesus Christ who created and has made us glorious, before all diligence in human affairs, and being further convinced that unity among the flocks of Christ is the preservation of ourselves and our subjects, the stout foundation and unshaken bulwark of our empire; being by these considerations moved with godly zeal, and offering to our God and Savior Jesus Christ the unity of the Holy Church as the first fruits of our reign, ordain that the basis and settlement of human felicity, namely, the symbol of the three hundred and eighteen holy fathers who were assembled, in concert with the Holy Spirit, at Nicæa, into which both ourselves and all our believing predecessors were baptized; that this alone should have reception and authority with the orthodox people in all the most holy churches of God, as the only formulary of the right faith, and sufficient for the utter destruction of every heresy, and for the complete unity of the holy churches of God; without prejudice, notwithstanding, to the force of the acts of the hundred and fifty holy fathers assembled in this imperial city, in confirmation of the sacred symbol itself, and in condemnation of those who blasphemed against the Holy Ghost; as well as of all that were passed in the metropolitan city of the Ephesians against the impious Nestorius and those who subsequently favored his opinions.

But the proceedings which have disturbed the unity and order of the holy churches of God, and the peace of the whole world, that is to say, the so-called tome of Leo, and all things said and done at Chalcedon in innovation upon the before-mentioned holy symbol of the three hundred and eighteen holy fathers, whether by way of definition of faith, or setting forth of symbols, or of interpretation, or instruction, or discourse; we ordain that these shall be anathematized both here and everywhere by the most holy bishops in every church, and shall be committed to the flames whenever they shall be found, inasmuch as it was so enjoined respecting all heretical doctrines by our predecessors, of pious and blessed memory, Constantine, and Theodosius the younger; and that, having thus been rendered null, they shall be utterly expelled from the one and only catholic and apostolic orthodox church, as superseding the everlasting and saving definitions of the three hundred and eighteen Fathers, and those of the blessed fathers who, by the Holy Spirit, made their decision at Ephesus; that no one, in short, either of the priesthood or laity, shall be allowed to deviate from that most sacred constitution of the holy symbol; and that, together with all the innovations upon the sacred symbol which were enacted at Chalcedon, there be also anathematized the heresy of those who do not confess, that the only begotten Son of God was truly incarnate, and made man of the Holy Spirit and of the Holy and ever-virgin Mary, Mother of God, but according to their strange conceit, either from heaven or in mere phantasy and seeming: and, in short, every heresy, and whatever other innovation, in respect either of thought or language, has been devised in violation of the sacred symbol in any manner or at any time or place.

And, inasmuch as it is the special task of kingly providence to furnish to their subjects with forecasting deliberation, abundant means of security, not only for the present but for future time to ordain that the most holy bishops in every place all subscribe to this our sacred circular epistle when exhibited to them, as a distinct declaration that they are indeed ruled by the sacred symbol of the three hundred and eighteen holy fathers alone—which the hundred and fifty holy fathers confirmed; as it was so defined by the most holy fathers, who, subsequently, assembled in the metropolitan city of the Ephesians, that the sacred symbol of the three hundred and eighteen holy fathers ought to be the only rule—while they anathematize every stumbling-block enacted at Chalcedon to the faith of the orthodox people, and utterly eject them from the churches, as an impediment to the general happiness and our own.

Those, moreover, who, after the issuing of these our sacred letters, which we trust to have been uttered in accordance with the will of God, in an endeavor to accomplish that unity which all desire for the holy churches of God, shall attempt to bring forward or so much as to name the innovation upon the faith which was enacted at Chalcedon, either in discourse or instruction or writing, in whatever manner, place, or time; with respect to those persons, as being the cause of confusion and tumult in the churches of God and among the whole of our subjects, and enemies to God and our safety, we command (in accordance with the laws ordained by our predecessor, Theodosius, of blessed and sacred memory, against such sort, of evil designs, which laws are subjoined to this our sacred circular) that, if

91

bishops or clergy, they be deposed; if monks or laics, that they be subjected to banishment, and every mode of confiscation, and the severest penalties for so the holy and homoousian Trinity, the Creator and Vivifier of the universe, which has ever been adored by our piety, receiving at the present time service at our hands in the destruction of the before-mentioned tares and the confirmation of the true and apostolic traditions of the holy symbol, and being thereby rendered favorable and gracious to our souls and to all our subjects, shall ever aid us in the exercise of our sway, and preserve the peace of the world."

CHAPTER V

RECEPTION OF THE CIRCULAR

According to Zacharias, the rhetorician, Timotheus who, as I said, was just returned from banishment, agrees to these circular letters; as does also Peter, president of the church of Antioch, surnamed the Fuller, who also attended Timotheus at the imperial city. After these proceedings, they also determined that Paul should occupy the archiepiscopal throne of the church of Ephesus. This author also says, that Anastasius, the successor of Juvenalis as president of Jerusalem, subscribes the circular, and very many others; so that those who repudiated the tome of Leo and the synod of Chalcedon, amounted to about five hundred: and also that a written petition was addressed to Basiliscus by the Asiatic bishops, assembled at Ephesus, a part of which is couched in the following terms:

"To our entirely pious and Christ-loving lords, Basiliscus and Marcus, ever victorious Emperors." Presently it proceeds: "Whenever the faith has been hated and assailed, you, all pious and Christ-loving sovereigns, have made it manifest throughout that you were equally assailed."

And further on: "A certain fearful retribution of judgment and fury of divine fire and the just wrath of your serenity shall suddenly involve the adversaries, those who endeavor with vauntful assault to battle down the mighty God and your sovereignty fortified by the faith; who also in various ways have not spared our humble selves, but have continually slandered and belied us, as having subscribed to your sacred and apostolic circular letters by compulsion and violence, which we, in fact, subscribed with all joy and readiness."

And further on: "Let it, therefore be your pleasure, that nothing be put forward otherwise than as accords with your sacred circular, being assured that, as we have before said, the whole world will be turned upside down, and the evils which have proceeded from the synod at Chalcedon will be found trifling in comparison, notwithstanding the innumerable slaughters which they have caused and the blood of the orthodox which they have unjustly and lawlessly shed."

And further on: "We conjure your piety, in the presence of our Lord Jesus Christ, to maintain the just and canonical and ecclesiastical condemnation and deposition which has been inflicted on them, and especially on him who has been on many points convicted of having unduly exercised the episcopate of the imperial city."

The same Zacharias also writes as follows: "On the issuing of the imperial circulars, those in the capital who were infected with the phantasy of Eutyches, and followed the monastic rule, believing themselves to have chanced on a prize in the person of Timotheus, and hoping by the circulars to catch their own profit, flock to him with all speed, and again retire, as if convinced by Timotheus that the Word of God is consubstantial with ourselves as to flesh, and consubstantial with the Father as respects the Godhead."

CHAPTER VI

PROCEEDINGS OF TIMOTHY ÆLURUS

The same author says that Timotheus, setting out from the imperial city, visited Ephesus, and there enthroned Paul as archpriest; who had already been ordained, according to the more ancient custom, by the bishops of the province, but had been ejected from his see: and he also restored to Ephesus the dignity of the patriarchate, of which the synod at Chalcedon had deprived it, as I have already mentioned. Proceeding thence, he arrives at Alexandria, and uniformly required all who approached him to anathematize the synod at Chalcedon. Accordingly, there abandon him, as has been recorded by the same Zacharias, many of his party, and among them Theodotus, one of the bishops ordained at Joppa by Theodosius, who had, by means of certain persons, become bishop of Jerusalem, at the time when Juvenalis betook himself to Byzantium.

CHAPTER VII

COUNTER CIRCULAR OF BASILISCUS

This author also says, that Acacius, president of the church of Constantinople, in consequence of these proceedings, stirred up the monastic body and the populace of the imperial city, on the plea that Basiliscus was a heretic: and that, the latter repudiated the circular, and issued a constitution to the effect, that transactions precipitated by overbearing influence were utterly null, and also sent forth a counter Circular in recommendation of the synod at Chalcedon. This counter circular as he terms it, he has, however, omitted, having written the whole work under passionate feelings. It is as follows:

THE COUNTER CIRCULAR OF BASILISCUS

"We, the emperors, Cæsars, Basiliscus and Marcus thus ordain: that the apostolic and orthodox faith, which has held sway in the catholic churches from the very first, both until the beginning and during the continuance of our reign, and ought to sway in all coming time, into which also we were baptized, and in which we believe; that this alone continue to sway uninjured and unshaken, and ever prevail throughout the catholic and apostolic churches of the orthodox and that no question tending otherwise be a subject of debate. On this account we also enjoin, that all acts during our reign, whether circular letters or others, or any thing whatever relating to faith or ecclesiastical constitution, be null; while we at the same time anathematize Nestorius, Eutyches, and every other heresy, with all who hold like sentiments; and that no synod or other debate be held on this subject, but that the present form remain unimpaired and unshaken. Also, that the provinces, the ordination to which was possessed by the see of this imperial and glorious city be restored to the most reverent and holy patriarch and archbishop Acacius, the present bishops, highly beloved of God, retaining their respective sees; provided that no prejudice thence arise after their demise to the right of ordination belonging to the illustrious see of this imperial and glorious city. That this our sacred ordinance has the force of a sacred constitution is a matter of doubt to none."

Such was the course of these transactions.

CHAPTER VIII
RESTORATION OF ZENO

AD 477

But Zeno, having seen in a vision the holy and much tried proto-martyr Thecla encouraging him and promising him restoration to power, after winning over the besiegers by bribes, marches on Byzantium and expels AD 477 Basiliscus, who had now held the supreme power for two years, and, on his taking refuge in a holy precinct, surrenders him to his enemies. Zeno, in consequence, dedicated to the proto-martyr Thecla a very extensive sanctuary, of singular stateliness and beauty, at Seleucia, which is situated near the borders of Isauria, and embellished it with very many and royal Offerings, which have been preserved to our times.

Basiliscus is, accordingly, conveyed to Cappadocia, in order to his death, and is slain with his wife and children at the station named Acusus. Zeno enacts a law in abrogation of what Basiliscus the tyrant had constituted by his circulars, and Peter, surnamed the Fuller, is ejected from the church of the Antiochenes, and Paul from that of the Ephesians.

CHAPTER IX

EPISTLE OF THE ASIATIC BISHOPS TO ACACIUS.

The bishops of Asia, to soothe Acacius, address to him a deprecatory plea, and implore his pardon in a repentant memorial, wherein they alleged that they had subscribed the circular by compulsion and not voluntarily; and they affirmed with an oath that the case was really thus, and that they had settled their faith, and still maintained it in accordance with the synod at Chalcedon. The purport of the document is as follows:

An epistle or petition sent from the bishops of Asia, to Acacius, bishop of Constantinople. "To Acacius, the most holy and pious patriarch of the church in the imperial city of Constantine, the New Rome," And it afterwards proceeds: "We have been duly visited by the person who will also act as our representative." And shortly after: "By these letters we acquaint you that we subscribed, not designedly but of necessity, having agreed to these matters with letters and words, not with the heart. For, by your acceptable prayers and the will of the higher Power, we hold the faith as we have received it from the three hundred and eighteen lights of the world, and the hundred and fifty holy fathers; and, moreover, we assent to the terms which were piously and rightly framed at Chalcedon by the holy fathers there assembled."

Whether Zacharias has slandered these persons, or they themselves lied in asserting that they were unwilling to subscribe, I am not able to say.

CHAPTER X
SUCCESSION OF BISHOPS AT ANTIOCH.

Next to Peter, Stephen succeeds to the see of Antioch, whom the sons of the Antiochenes dispatched with reeds sharpened like lances, as is recorded by John the Rhetorician. After Stephen, Calandion is entrusted with the helm of that see, and he wrought upon those who approached him, to anathematize Timotheus, and, at the same time, the circular of Basiliscus.

CHAPTER XI
SUCCESSION OF BISHOPS AT ALEXANDRIA.

It was the intention of Zeno to eject Timotheus from the church of Alexandria; but, on being informed by certain persons that he was already aged, and had almost reached the common resting-place of all men, he abandoned his purpose. And, in fact, Timotheus shortly after paid the debt of nature. Upon this the Alexandrian bishops elect, on their own authority, Peter, surnamed Mongus; the announcement of which proceeding exasperated Zeno, who judged him to have incurred the penalty of death, and he recalled Timotheus, the successor of Proterius, while residing, on account of a popular tumult, at Canopus. Thus, Timotheus obtained, by the commands of the emperor, possession of his rightful see.

CHAPTER XII
ECCLESIASTICAL MEASURES OF ZENO.

By the advice of certain persons, John, a presbyter, who held the office of steward of the venerable temple of the holy forerunner and baptist John, visits the imperial city, in order to negotiate permission for the inhabitants of Alexandria to elect as president of their church a person of their own choice, if it should happen that their bishop should depart out of the world. According to Zacharias, he was detected by the emperor in the endeavor to compass his own appointment to the bishopric, and was allowed to return home, under an oath that he would never aspire to the see of Alexandria. The emperor too issues a precept, to the effect that, after the death of Timotheus, that person should be bishop whom the clergy and people might elect. On the death of Timotheus, which took place shortly after, John, by the employment of money, as the same Zacharias writes, and in disregard of his sworn pledge to the emperor, procures his own nomination as bishop of the Alexandrians. The emperor, on being informed of these circumstances, commands his expulsion, and, at the suggestion

AD 482 of certain persons, addresses and allocution to the Alexandrians, which he named Henoticon, directing, at the same time, that the see of Alexandria should be restored to Peter, with a stipulation, that he should subscribe this document and admit to communion the party of Proterius.

CHAPTER XIII

PUBLICATION OF THE HENOTICON OF ZENO.

Of this measure of arrangement, framed according to the advice of Acacius, bishop of the imperial city, Pergamius is the bearer, who had been appointed procurator of Egypt. Finding, on his arrival at Alexandria, that John had fled, he addresses himself to Peter, and urges him to receive the allocution of Zeno, and also to admit the separatists. He, accordingly, receives and subscribes the before mentioned allocution, with a promise also to admit to communion the members of the opposite party. Accordingly, on occasion of a general festival at Alexandria and the universal acceptance of the so-called Henoticon of Zeno, Peter admits the partisans of Proterius; and, on delivering in the church an address to the people, he reads the allocution of Zeno as follows.

CHAPTER XIV

THE HENOTICON (INSTRUMENT OF UNION).

"The emperor Cæsar Zeno, pious, victorious, triumphant, supreme, ever worshipful Augustus, to the most reverent bishops and clergy, and to the monks and laity throughout Alexandria, Egypt, Libya, and Pentapolis. Being assured that the origin and constitution, the might and invincible defense of our sovereignty is the only right and true faith, which, through divine inspiration, the three hundred holy fathers assembled at Nicæa set forth, and the hundred and fifty holy fathers, who in like manner met at Constantinople, confirmed; we night and day employ every means of prayer, of zealous pains and of laws, that the holy Catholic and apostolic church in every place may be multiplied, the uncorruptible and immortal mother of our scepter; and that the pious laity, continuing in peace and unanimity with respect to God, may, together with the bishops, highly beloved of God, the most pious clergy, the archimandrites and monks, offer up acceptably their supplications in behalf of our sovereignty. So long as our great God and Savior Jesus Christ, who was incarnate and born of Mary, the Holy Virgin, and Mother of God, approves and readily accepts our concordant glorification and service, the power of our enemies will be crushed and swept away, and peace with its blessings, kindly temperature, abundant produce, and whatever is beneficial to man, will be liberally bestowed.

Since, then, the irreprehensible faith is the preserver both of ourselves and the Roman weal, petitions have been offered to us from pious archimandrites and hermits, and other venerable persons, imploring us with tears that unity should be procured for the churches, and the limbs should be knit together, which the enemy of all good has of old time been eagerly bent upon severing, under a consciousness that defeat will befall him whenever he assails the body while in an entire condition. For since it happens, that of the unnumbered generations which during the lapse of so many years time has withdrawn from life, some have departed, deprived of the laver of regeneration, and others have been borne away on the inevitable journey of man, without having partaken in the divine communion; and innumerable murders have also been perpetrated; and not only the earth, but the very air has been defiled by a multitude of blood-sheddings; that this state of things might be transformed into good, who would not pray?

For this reason, we were anxious that you should be informed, that we and the churches in every quarter neither have held, nor do we or shall we hold, nor are we aware of persons who hold, any other symbol or lesson or definition of faith or creed than the beforementioned holy symbol of the three hundred and eighteen holy fathers, which the aforesaid hundred and fifty holy fathers confirmed; and if any person does hold such, we deem him an alien: for we are confident that this symbol alone is, as we said, the preserver of our sovereignty, and on their reception of this alone are all the people baptized when desirous of the saving illumination: which symbol all the holy fathers assembled at Ephesus also followed; who further passed sentence of deposition on the impious Nestorius and those who subsequently held his sentiments: which Nestorius we also anathematize, together with Eutyches and all who entertain opinions contrary to those above-mentioned, receiving at the same time the twelve chapters of Cyril, of holy memory, formerly archbishop of the holy Catholic church of the Alexandrians.

We moreover confess, that the only begotten Son of God, himself God, who truly assumed manhood, namely, our Lord Jesus Christ, who is consubstantial with the Father in respect of the Godhead, and consubstantial with ourselves as respects the manhood; that He, having descended, and become incarnate of the Holy Spirit and Mary, the Virgin and Mother of God, is one and not two; for we affirm that both his miracles, and the sufferings which he voluntarily endured in the flesh, are those of a single person: for we do in no degree admit those who either make a division or a confusion, or introduce a phantom; inasmuch as his truly sinless incarnation from the Mother of God did not produce an addition of a son, because the Trinity continued a Trinity even when one member of the Trinity, the God Word, became incarnate.

Knowing, then, that neither the holy orthodox churches of God in all parts, nor the priests, highly beloved of God, who are at their head, nor our own sovereignty, have allowed or do allow any other symbol or definition of faith than the beforementioned holy lesson, we have united ourselves thereto without hesitation. And these things we write not as setting forth a new form of faith, but for your assurance: and every one who has held or holds any other opinion, either at the present or another time, whether at Chalcedon or in any synod whatever, we anathematize; and specially the before-mentioned Nestorius and Eutyches, and those who maintain their doctrines.

Link yourselves, therefore, to the spiritual mother, the church, and in her enjoy the same communion with us, according to the aforesaid one and only definition of the faith, namely, that of the three hundred and eighteen holy fathers. For your all holy mother, the church, waits to embrace you as true children, and longs to hear your loved voice, so long withheld. Speed yourselves, therefore, for by so doing you will both draw towards yourselves the favor of our Master and Savior and God, Jesus Christ, and be commended by out sovereignty."

When this had been read, all the Alexandrians united themselves to the holy catholic and apostolic church.

CHAPTER XV

CORRESPONDENCE BETWEEN SIMPLICIUS AND ZENO.

John, however, of whom we have made mention before, having fled from Alexandria, arrives at the ancient Rome, and there causes great stir by saying that he had been banished from his rightful see for upholding the doctrines of Leo and the council at Chalcedon, and had been superseded by another person who was their opponent. Upon this Simplicius, bishop of the elder Rome, writes in alarm to Zeno; who in reply charges John with perjury, and alleges that for this reason and no other he had been ejected from his bishopric.

CHAPTER XVI

DEPOSITION OF CALANDION AND RESTORATION OF PETER THE FULLER.

Calandion, president of Antioch, writing to the emperor Zeno, and to Acacius, president of Constantinople, terms Peter an adulterer, saying that when he was at Alexandria, he had anathematized the council at Chalcedon. He is afterwards condemned to exile at Oasis, on a supposition of having supported Illus, Leontius, and Pamprepius, in their usurpation against Zeno; and Peter the Fuller, the predecessor of Calandion and Stephen, as I have mentioned, recovered his own see. The latter also subscribed the Henoticon of Zeno, and addressed synodical letters to Peter, bishop of Alexandria. Acacius, president of Constantinople, also entered into communion with him. Martyrius, too, bishop of Jerusalem, addressed synodical letters to Peter. Subsequently, certain persons withdrew from communion with Peter, who, in consequence, thenceforward openly anathematized the synod at Chalcedon. The news of this circumstance greatly troubled

Acacius, and induced him to send persons to gain information on the subject; when Peter, to convince them that he had not so acted, drew up memorials, in which certain persons said, from their own knowledge, that Peter had not done any thing of the kind.

CHAPTER XVII

LETTER FROM PETER TO ACACIUS.

This Peter never abided by one opinion, being a double dealer, a waverer, and a time-server, now anathematizing the synod at Chalcedon, at another time recanting, and admitting it with entire assent. Accordingly, the same Peter wrote an epistle to Acacius, president of Constantinople, in the following words:

"The most high God will repay your holiness for the many labors and toils wherewith, during the lapse of time, you have guarded the form of the faith of the holy fathers; in which form hen we found the symbol of the three hundred and eighteen holy fathers to be embraced, we were disposed to accord with it; that symbol in which we believed at baptism, and still believe; which also the hundred and fifty holy fathers, who assembled at Constantinople, confirmed.

"Accordingly, while increasing in your endeavors to guide all aright, you have united the holy church of God, by convincing us by the most powerful proofs that nothing at variance with this was enacted in the holy and general synod held at Chalcedon, but that it accorded with the acts of the holy fathers at Nicæa, and confirmed them. Thus, having discovered no novelty therein, we have of our own free motion accorded our assent and belief. But we are informed that certain monks, envying our brotherly union, have conveyed certain slanders to your holy ears, which have with some difficulty succeeded in embittering the feelings of your holiness. And, in the first place it is alleged that we have removed to another place the remains of our sainted father, the blessed archbishop Timotheus, a thing abhorrent to religion and law: and they have further shifted their ground to another charge, in itself incoherent and worse than the former; for how could we possibly have anathematized the synod at Chalcedon which we had previously confirmed by according to it our belief? But the malignant temper and fickleness of our people are notorious, and cannot but be known to your piety, as well as of those monks who are disposed to innovation; who in conspiracy with certain ill-designing persons that have broken loose from the church, are endeavoring to draw away the people. Through your prayers we have also devised a discourse of a directly healing tendency, and in no way impugning the synod at Chalcedon, well knowing that its transactions contain no novelty; and, further, for the satisfaction of guileless persons, we have procured those who had united themselves to us, to affirm this point.

"This mischief, then, by much exertion, I have readily checked: but I make known to your holiness, that even still the monks who are ever sowing the tares, are not at rest, associating also with themselves, as instruments, persons who were never the inmates of monasteries; but they travel about disseminating various rumors to our disadvantage, and while they do not allow that we act canonically and in a manner suitable to the holy catholic church of God, but are habituating our people to govern rather than obey us, they are bent on doing whatever is unbecoming the service of God. We doubt not, however, that your holiness will inform the most sacred master of the world of all these circumstances, and provide that a formulary shall be put forth by his serenity, embracing the necessary matters relating to such a peace of the church as becomes both God and the emperor; so as to lead all to repose on its provisions."

CHAPTER XVIII

FELIX ISSUES A SENTENCE OF DEPOSITION
AGAINST ACACIUS.

Pope Felix III
483-492

John, who had fled to Rome, was urgent on Felix the successor
of Simplicius in that see, respecting the proceedings of Peter,
and recommends, according to Zacharias, that an instrument
of deposition should be sent to Acacius from Felix, on the
ground of his communion with Peter: which, however,
as being uncanonical, Acacius did not admit, as the same
Zacharias writes, on its presentation by certain members of
the monastery of the Acoemets, as they are called. Such is
the account given by Zacharias; but he appears to me to have
been altogether ignorant of the real transactions, and to have
reported merely an imperfect hearsay. I now proceed to give
a precise account of the proceedings. On the presentation
of libels to Felix by John against Acacius, on the score of
irregular communion with Peter, and other uncanonical
proceedings, the bishops Vitalis and Misenus are sent by
Felix to the emperor Zeno, with a requisition that the authority
of the synod at Chalcedon should be maintained, that Peter
should be ejected as a heretic, and that Acacius should be sent
to Felix to answer for himself to the charges brought against
him by John, of whom we have made frequent mention.

CHAPTER XIX

INTERFERENCE OF CYRIL THE MONK.

Before, however, they reached the imperial city, Cyril, the
superior of the Acoemets, writes to Felix, blaming his tardiness,
when so grievous offenses were being committed against the
right faith; and Felix writes to Misenus and his associates, that
they should take no measures until they had conferred with
Cyril, and learnt from him what was best to be done.

105

CHAPTER XX

CORRESPONDENCE BETWEEN FELIX AND ZENO.

Further commonitories were also addressed to them by Felix; as also letters to Zeno, concerning both the synod at Chalcedon, and the persecution which Huneric was carrying on in Africa. He also wrote an epistle to Acacius. Zeno wrote in answer, that the concern with which John had filled him, was groundless; because, having sworn that he would in no way endeavor to insinuate himself into the see of Alexandria, and having subsequently violated these terms and disregarded his oath, he had been guilty of the extreme of sacrilege: that Peter had not been appointed without being tested, but had with his own hand subscribed his reception of the faith of the three hundred and eighteen holy fathers who met at Nicæa, which the holy synod at Chalcedon also followed. Part of the epistle is in these precise words:

"You ought to be assured that our piety, and the before-mentioned most holy Peter, and all the most holy churches, receive and revere the most holy synod at Chalcedon, which agreed with the faith of the Nicene synod."

In the transactions are also contained epistles from the before-mentioned Cyril, and other archimandrites of the imperial city, and from bishops and clergy of the Egyptian province, addressed to Felix against Peter, as being a heretic, and against those who communicated with him. The members of the monastery of the Acoemets who came to Felix, further averred against Misenus and his party, that before their arrival at Byzantium, the name of Peter had been read secretly in the sacred diptychs, and since that time without any concealment, and that they had in this way communicated with him. The epistle also of the Egyptians affirmed the same things respecting Peter; and that John, being orthodox, had been rightfully ordained: that Peter was ordained by two bishops only, maintainers of similar errors with himself: that since the flight of John every species of severity had been inflicted on the orthodox: that all these circumstances had been made known to Acacius by persons who had visited the imperial city; and that they were convinced that he was in all things acting in union with Peter.

CHAPTER XXI

ACCUSATION OF THE LEGATES BY SIMEON THE MONK, AND THEIR CONSEQUENT DEPRIVATION.

This stir was further increased by Simeon, an Acoemet, who had been dispatched to Rome by Cyril. He expressly charged Misenus and Vitalis with holding communion with the heretics, by distinctly uttering the name of Peter in the reading of the sacred diptychs; and affirmed that many simple persons had, on this ground, been beguiled by the heretics, who said that Peter was admitted to the communion even of the Roman see: and, further, in reply to various interrogatories, Simeon said that Misenus and his party had declined to have communication with any orthodox person, either in person or by letter, or to sift any of the presumptuous attempts upon the right faith. There was also brought forward Silvanus, a presbyter, who had been in company with Misenus and Vitalis at Constantinople, and he confirmed the statement of the monks. There was read, too, a letter from Acacius: to Simplicius, to the effect that Peter had been long ago deposed and had become a child of night.

On these grounds Misenus and Vitalis were removed from the priesthood and severed from the holy communion, when a unanimous vote was passed by the synod, in the following terms: "The church of the Romans does not admit Peter, the heretic, who has also been long ago condemned by the holy see, excommunicated, and anathematized. To whom, if there were no other objection this is sufficient, namely, that having been ordained by heretics, he could not have authority over the orthodox."

The decree also contains what follows: "The mere circumstance shows Acacius, bishop of Constantinople, to have incurred very great responsibility, because, writing to Simplicius and having termed Peter a heretic, he has nevertheless made no such declaration to the emperor: which was his duty if he were loyal to him. He is, however, more partial to the emperor than to the faith."

Let me now return to the order of events. There is extant an epistle from Acacius to the Egyptian bishops, the clergy, monks, and the people in general by which he endeavors to heal the existing schism on which subject he also wrote to Peter, bishop of Alexandria.

CHAPTER XXII

COMMOTION AT ALEXANDRIA ON ACCOUNT OF THE COUNCIL OF CHALCEDON.

While the schism at Alexandria was thus at its height, Peter, having again anathematized the tome of Leo, the transactions at Chalcedon, and those who refused to admit the writings of Dioscorus and Timotheus, induced some of the bishops and archimandrites to communicate with him, and failing to prevail upon the others, ejected most of them from their monasteries. On account of these proceedings, Nephalius visited the imperial city, and reported them to Zeno; who, in great vexation, despatches Cosmas, one of his officers, charged to load Peter with menaces, for the enforcement of unity, on the score of his having caused a serious dissension by his harshness. Cosmas returns to the imperial city without accomplishing the object of his mission, having merely restored those who had been ejected to their monasteries.

Subsequently, Arsenius is sent out by the emperor as governor of Egypt and commander of the forces. Arriving at

Alexandria in company with Nephalius, he negotiated with a view to unity; but failing to induce persons to acquiesce in his measures, he sends some of them to the imperial city, where, accordingly, many discussions took place in the presence of Zeno: but with no practical result, because the emperor altogether declined agreement with the synod at Chalcedon.

CHAPTER XXIII

SUCCESSION OF BISHOPS AT CONSTANTINOPLE, ALEXANDRIA, AND ANTIOCH.

At this juncture Acacius departed on the common journey of all men, and is succeeded by Fravitas. On his addressing synodical letters to Peter of Alexandria, the latter replies with a repetition of the former matters respecting the synod at Chalcedon. On the demise of Fravitas, after an episcopate of only four months, Euphemius was ordained as his successor, and is the recipient of the letters of Peter addressed to Fravitas. On discovering the anathema against the transactions at Chalcedon, his feelings were greatly roused, and he broke off from communion with Peter. Both epistles are extant, namely, from Fravitas to Peter, and from Peter to Fravitas; but I pass them over on account of their length.

When, in consequence, Euphemius and Peter were upon the point of coming to open hostility, and summoning synods against each other, these proceedings were prevented by the death of the latter. He is succeeded by Athanasius, who attempted to unite the dissidents; but without success, since the parties were ranged under differences of opinion. Subsequently, when dispatching synodical letters to Palladius, the successor of Peter in the bishopric of Antioch, he took a similar course respecting the synod at Chalcedon; as did also John, his successor in the see of Alexandria.

On the death of Palladius, and the succession of Flavian to the see of Antioch, Solomon, a presbyter of that church, is sent to Alexandria, as the bearer of synodical letters, with the request of an answer from John to Flavian. John is succeeded in the see of Alexandria by another of the same name. Such was the progress of these events down to a certain period of the reign of Anastasius: who had himself ejected Euphemius. I have been compelled thus to detail them continuously, for the sake of perspicuity and a ready comprehension of the whole.

CHAPTER XXIV

DEATH OF ARMATUS.

Zeno, at the instigation of Illus, puts to death Armatus, a kinsman of the empress Verina. When Armatus had been sent against him by Basiliscus, Zeno had succeeded, by bribes, in converting him from a foe into an ally and had bestowed on his son Basiliscus the rank of Cæsar at Nicæa: but on his return to Constantinople, he procures the assassination of Armatus, and makes his son a priest instead of Cæsar. The latter was afterwards raised to the episcopal dignity.

CHAPTER XXV

INSURRECTION AND DEATH OF THEODORIC.

Theodoric also, a Scythian, raised an insurrection, and having collected his forces in Thrace, marched against Zeno. After ravaging every place in his march as far as the mouth of the Pontus, he was near taking the imperial city, when some of his most intimate companions were secretly induced to enter into a plot against his life. When, however, he had learnt the disaffection of his followers, he commenced a retreat, and was very soon afterwards numbered with the departed, by a kind of death which I will mention, and which happened thus. A spear, with its thong prepared for immediate use, had been suspended before his tent in barbaric fashion. He had ordered a horse to be brought to him for the purpose of exercise, and being in the habit of not having any one to assist him in mounting, vaulted into his seat. The horse, a mettlesome and ungovernable animal, reared before Theodoric was fairly mounted, so that, in the contest, neither daring to rein back the horse, lest it should come down upon him, nor yet having gained a firm seat, he was whirled round in all directions, and dashed against the point of the spear, which thus struck him obliquely, and wounded his side. He was then conveyed to his couch, and after surviving a few days, died of the wound.

CHAPTER XXVI

INSURRECTION OF MARCIAN.

Subsequently Marcian had a rupture with Zeno, and attempted to dispute the empire with him. He was the son of Anthemius who had formerly reigned at Rome, and was allied to Leo, the preceding emperor, having married his younger daughter Leontia. After a severe battle around the palace, in which many fell on both sides, Marcian repulsed his opponents, and would have become master of the palace, had he not let slip the critical moment, by putting off the operation to the morrow.

For the critical season[2] is swift of flight: when it is close upon one, it may be secured; but should it once have escaped the grasp, it soars aloft and laughs at its pursuers, not deigning to place itself again within their reach. And hence no doubt it is, that statuaries and painters, while they figure it with a lock hanging down in front, represent the head as closely shaven behind; thus skillfully symbolizing, that when it comes up from behind one, it may perhaps be held fast by the flowing forelock, but fairly escapes when it has once got the start, from the absence of any thing by which the pursuer might grasp it.

And this was what befell Marcian, when he had lost the moment favorable to his success, and was unable to find it afterwards. For the next day he was betrayed by his own followers, and being completely deserted, fled to the sacred precinct of the divine Apostles; whence he was dragged away by force, and transported to Cæsarea in Cappadocia. Having there joined the society of certain monks, he was afterwards detected in meditating an escape; and being removed by the emperor to Tarsus in Cilicia, he was shorn, and ordained a presbyter: of all which particulars an elegant narrative has been given by Eustathius the Syrian.

CHAPTER XXVII

INSURRECTION OF ILLUS AND LEONTIUS.

The same writer states that Zeno also devised innumerable machinations against his mother-in-law Verina, and afterwards sent her away to Cilicia; and that subsequently, on the assumption of sovereign power by Illus, she removed to what is called the castle of Papirius; where she died.

Eustathius also narrates with great ability the story of Illus: how he escaped Zeno's plots against him, and how Zeno gave up to capital punishment the man who had been commissioned to murder Illus, rewarding him with the loss of his head for his failure in the attempt. He also appointed Illus commander of the forces of the East, thinking thus to conceal his real designs: but he, having gained over as partisans Leontius, Marsus, a man of reputation, and Pamprepius, proceeded to the east.

The same Eustathius then mentions the proclamation of Leontius as emperor, which took place at Tarsus in Cilicia; and how these persons reaped the fruits of their assumption of power, when Theodoric, a man of Gothic extraction, but illustrious among the Romans, had been sent out against them, with a force composed both of native and foreign troops.

The same author ably depicts the fate of those who were miserably put to death by Zeno in return for their loyalty to him; and how Theodoric, becoming aware of the evil designs of Zeno, withdrew to the elder Rome. Some, however, say that this was done at the suggestion of Zeno. Having there defeated Odoacer, he made himself master of Rome, and assumed the title of king.

CHAPTER XXVIII

ACCOUNT OF MAMMIANUS AND HIS STRUCTURES.

John the rhetorician writes that in the time of Zeno, Mammianus from an artisan became a person of note and a member of the senate; and that he built in the suburb of Daphne what is called the Antiphorus on a site previously planted with vines and suitable for cultivation, directly opposite the public baths; where there is also the brazen statue inscribed, "Mammianus, the friend of the city." He also states that he built within the city, two basilicas, singularly beautiful in their design, and embellished with brilliant stone-work; and that, as an intervening structure to the two, he raised a Tetrapylum, exquisitely finished both in its columns and its brazen work. The basilicas I have identified, retaining, together with their name, some trace of their former beauty, in the stones from Proconnesus, which form the pavement, but nothing remarkable in their architecture: for, in consequence of the calamities which had befallen them, they had, lately been rebuilt, without receiving any thing in the way of ornament. Of the Tetrapylum I was not able to detect the slightest vestige.

CHAPTER XXIX

DEATH OF ZENO. SUCCESSION OF ANASTASIUS.

On the decease of Zeno, by epilepsy, without issue; after a reign of seventeen years, Longinus his brother, having raised himself to considerable power, hoped to secure the sovereignty, but was, notwithstanding, disappointed of his expectation. For Ariadne bestows the diadem on

AD 491

Anastasius, a person who had not yet attained senatorian rank, but belonged to the corps of the Silentiaries.

Eustathius writes that two hundred and seven years elapsed from the beginning of the reign of Diocletian to the death of Zeno and the nomination of Anastasius: five hundred and fifty-two years and seven months from the time that Augustus obtained the supreme power; eight hundred and thirty-two years and seven months from the reign of Alexander the Macedonian; one thousand and fifty-two years and seven months from the reign of Romulus; one thousand six hundred and eighty-six years and seven months from the taking of Troy.

This Anastasius, being a native of Epidamnus, now called Dyrrachium, both succeeds to the sovereignty of Zeno and espouses his wife Ariadne. In the first place, he dismisses to his native country Longinus, the brother of Zeno, who held the post of Master of the Offices, formerly termed commander of the household troops; and afterwards, many other Isaurians at their own request.

CHAPTER XXX

DIVISIONS IN THE CHURCH.

This Anastasius, being of a peaceful disposition, was altogether averse to the introduction of changes, especially in the state of the church, but endeavored by every means, that the most holy churches should continue undisturbed, and the whole body of his subjects enjoy profound tranquillity, by the removal of all strife and contention from matters both ecclesiastical and civil. During these times, accordingly, the synod of Chalcedon was neither openly proclaimed in the most holy churches, nor yet was repudiated by all: but the bishops acted each according to his individual opinion, Thus, some very resolutely maintained what had been put forth by that synod, and would not yield to the extent of one word of its determinations, nor admit even the change of a single letter, but firmly declined all contact and communion with those who refused to admit the matters there set forth. Others, again, not only did not submit to the synod of Chalcedon and its determinations, but even anathematized both it and the tome of Leo. Others, however, firmly adhered to the Henoticon of Zeno, and that too although mutually at variance on the point of the single and double nature; some being caught by the artful composition of that document; and others influenced by an inclination for peace.

Thus the churches in general were divided into distinct factions, and their presidents did not even admit each other to communion. Numerous divisions, hence arising, existed in the East, in the West, and in Africa; while the eastern bishops had no friendly intercourse with those of the West and Africa, nor the latter with those of the East. The evil too became still more monstrous, for neither did the presidents of the eastern churches allow communion among themselves, nor yet those who held the sees of Europe and Africa, much less with those of remote parts.

In consideration of these circumstances, the Emperor Anastasius removed those bishops who were promoters of change, wherever he detected any one either proclaiming or anathematizing the synod of Chalcedon in opposition to the practice of the neighborhood. Accordingly, he rejected from the see of the imperial city, first, Euphemius, as has been already mentioned, and afterwards Macedonius, who was succeeded by Timotheus: and Flavian from the see of Antioch.

CHAPTER XXXI

LETTER TO ALCISON FROM THE MONKS OF PALESTINE.

The monastic body in Palestine, writing to Alcison concerning Macedonius and Flavian, express themselves thus: "On the death of Peter, they were again separated, but Alexandria, Egypt, and Africa remained at unity among themselves; as, on the other hand, did the rest of the East; while the churches of the West refuse to communicate with them on any other terms than the anathematizing of Nestorius, Eutyches, and Dioscorus, including also Peter, surnamed Mongus, and Acacius.

"Such, then, being the situation of the churches throughout the world, the genuine followers of Dioscorus and Eutyches were reduced to a very small number; and when they were upon the point of disappearing altogether from the earth, Xenaias, who was truly a stranger to God, with what object we know not, or pursuing what enmity towards Flavian, but under color of defending the faith, as is generally said, begins to raise a stir against him, and to calumniate him as being a Nestorian. When, however, he had anathematized Nestorius and his notion, Xenaias transferred his attacks from him to Dioscorus and Theodore, Theodoret, Ibas, Cyrus, Eleutherius, and John; and we know not whom besides and whence he mustered them: some of whom really maintained the opinions of Nestorius, but others, having been suspected, anathematized him, and departed in the communion of the church. 'Unless,' said he, 'thou shalt anathematize all these, as holding the opinions of Nestorius, thou art thyself a Nestorian, though thou shouldest ten thousand times anathematize him and his notion.'

"He also endeavored by letters to induce the advocates of Dioscorus and Eutyches to take arms with him against Flavian, not however with a view exacting from him an anathema upon the synod, but merely on the before-mentioned persons. But when the bishop Flavian had maintained a prolonged resistance to them, and other persons had united with Xenaias against him, namely, Eleusinus, a bishop of Cappadocia Secunda, Nicias, of Laodicea in Syria, and others from other quarters, the motive of whose spite against Flavian it is the province of others, not of ourselves, to detail; at last, in hope of peace, he yielded to their contentious spirit, and having in writing anathematized the before-mentioned persons, he despatched the instrument to the emperor, for they had stirred up him also against Flavian as a maintainer of the opinions of Nestorius.

"Xenaias, not contented with this, again demands of Flavian that he should anathematize the synod itself, and those who maintained two natures in the person of the Lord, namely, the flesh and the Godhead; and on his refusal, again accused him of being a Nestorian. After much stir upon this subject, and after the patriarch had put forth an exposition of faith, in which he confessed that he admitted the synod as far as regards the deposition of Nestorius and Eutyches, not however as defining and teaching the faith; they again impugn him as secretly holding the opinions of Nestorius, unless he would further anathematize the synod itself, and those who maintained two natures in the person of the Lord, the flesh and the Godhead.

"They also win over to their side the Isaurians, by various deceitful expressions, and having drawn up a formulary of faith, in which they anathematize the synod together with those who maintained the two natures or persons, they separate themselves from Flavian and Macedonius, but unite with others on their subscribing the formulary. At the same time they also demanded of the bishop of Jerusalem a written statement of faith; which he put forth, and sent to the emperor by the hands of the party of Dioscorus. This they present, containing an anathema upon those who maintained the two natures. But the bishop of Jerusalem himself, affirming that it had been forged by them, puts forth another without such anathema. And no wonder. For they have often forged discourses of the fathers, and to many writings of Apollinaris they have attached titles assigning them to Athanasius, Gregory Thaumaturgus, and Julius; their principal object in so doing being to draw over the multitude to their own impieties.

"They also demanded of Macedonius a written statement of faith who put one forth, affirming that he recognized only the creed of the three hundred and eighteen, and of the one hundred and fifty fathers, anathematizing at the same time Nestorius, Eutyches, and those who held the doctrine of two sons or two Christs, or divided the natures; making, however, no mention of the synod of Ephesus, which deposed Nestorius, nor that of Chalcedon, which deposed Eutyches. Indignant at this, the monastic bodies about Constantinople separate from their bishop Macedonius. In the mean time Xenaias and Dioscorus, associating with them many of the bishops, became insufferable, from the stir which they raised against those who refused to anathematize; and by various devices, they endeavored to procure the banishment of those who persisted in their refusal. In this way, accordingly, they banish both Macedonius, and John, bishop of Paltus, and Flavian."

Such are the contents of the letter.

CHAPTER XXXII

EJECTION OF MACEDONIUS AND FLAVIAN FROM THEIR SEES.

There were other things which caused secret vexation to Anastasius. For when Ariadne was desirous of investing him with the purple, Euphemius, who held the archiepiscopal see, withheld his approval until Anastasius had presented to him an agreement, written with his own hand and secured with fearful oaths, that he would maintain the faith inviolate, and introduce no innovation into the holy church of God, in case he should obtain the scepter: which document he also deposited with Macedonius, the keeper of the sacred treasures. This measure he adopted, because Anastasius had generally the reputation of holding the Manichæan doctrine. When, however, Macedonius ascended the episcopal throne, Anastasius was desirous that the agreement should be returned to him, affirming it to be an insult to the imperial dignity, if the before-mentioned document, in his own hand-writing should be preserved: and when Macedonius resolutely opposed the demand, and firmly protested that he would not betray the faith, the emperor pursued every insidious device for the purpose of ejecting him from his see.

Accordingly, even boys were brought forward as informers, who falsely accused both themselves and Macedonius of infamous practices. But when Macedonius was found to be emasculate, they had recourse to other contrivances; until, by the advice of Celer, commander of the household troops, he secretly retired from his see.

With the ejection of Flavian, other circumstances are associated. For we have met with some very aged men who remembered all the events of this time. These say, that the monks of the district called Cynegica, and of the whole of Syria Prima, having been wrought upon by Xenaias, who was bishop of the neighboring city of Hierapolis, and who was named in Greek Philoxenus, rushed into the city in a body with great noise and tumult, endeavoring to compel Flavian to anathematize the synod of Chalcedon and the tome of Leo. Roused at the indignation manifested by Flavian, and the violent urgency of the monks, the people of the city made a great slaughter of them, so that a very large number found a grave in the Orontes where the waves performed their only funeral rites. There happened also another circumstance of scarcely less magnitude than the former. For the monks of Cæle Syria, now called Syria Secunda, from sympathy with Flavian, since he had led a monastic life in a monastery of the district called Tilmognon, advanced to Antioch, with the intention of defending him. From which circumstance, also, no inconsiderable mischief arose. Accordingly, on the ground either of the former or latter occurrence, or both, Flavian is ejected, and condemned to reside at Petra, on the extreme verge of Palestine.

CHAPTER XXXIII

SEVERUS BISHOP OF ANTIOCH.

Flavian having been thus ejected, Severus ascends the episcopal throne of Antioch, in the five hundred and sixty-first year of the era of that city, in the month Dius, the sixth year of the Indiction;

the year in which I am now writing being the six hundred and forty-first of that era. He was a native of Sozopolis, a city of Pisidia, and had applied himself to the profession of a pleader at Berytus; but immediately on his abandoning the practice of the law, having participated in holy baptism in the sacred precinct of the divine martyr Leontius, who is revered at Tripolis, a city of Phœnicia Maritima, he assumed the monastic life, in a certain monastery situated between the city of Gaza and the town called Majumas; in which latter place Peter the Iberian, who had been bishop of the same Gaza, and had been banished with Timotheus Ælurus, passed through the same discipline, and left behind him a famous memory. Severus there engages in a discussion with Nephalius, who had formerly sided with him on the question of the single nature, but had subsequently been one of the synod at Chalcedon and among those who held the opinion of two natures in the person of our Lord Jesus Christ; and he is, in consequence expelled from his own monastery by Nephalius and his party, together with many others who held similar doctrines. Thence he proceeds to the imperial city to plead the cause of himself and those who had be expelled with him, and thus obtains the notice of the emperor Anastasius, as is narrated by the author of the life of Severus.

Accordingly, Severus, in issuing synodical letters, expressly anathematized the synod at Chalcedon; on which point the letters addressed to Alcison speak as follows: "The synodical letters of Timotheus of Constantinople were admitted here in Palestine, but the deposition of Macedonius and Flavian was not admitted nor yet the synodical letters of Severus; but the bearers were put to flight, with the ignominy and insult which they deserved, by the people and monks of the city, who rose upon them. Such was the situation of matters in Palestine. But of the bishops subject to Antioch, some were carried away into compliance, among whom was Marinus, bishop of Berytus; others by force and compulsion concurred in the synodical letters of Severus, which included an anathema, both on the synod and all others who affirmed two natures or persons in the Lord, namely, the flesh and the Godhead; and others, after having concurred by compulsion, recalled their assent, and among them the bishops subject to Apamea; others, again, altogether refused concurrence, among whom were Julian, bishop of Bostra, Epiphanius of Tyre, and some others, as is said. But the Isaurian bishops, having returned to their sober senses, are now condemning themselves for the error into which they had been beguiled, and are anathematizing Severus and his party. Others of the bishops and clergy subject to Severus have abandoned their churches, and among them Julian of Bostra, and Peter of Damascus, who are now living in these parts, as also Mamas. This latter is one of those two who seemed to be the chiefs of the followers of Dioscorus, by whose means also Severus obtained his dignity: but he now condemns the arrogance of that party."

And presently the letter proceeds. "The monasteries in these parts and Jerusalem itself are, with the aid of God, unanimous respecting the right faith, and very many cities besides, together with their bishops, for all of whom, and for ourselves, pray thou that we may not enter into temptation, our most holy lord and honored father."

CHAPTER XXXIV

ACT OF DEPOSITION AGAINST SEVERUS.

Since, then, these letters state that the priests subject to Apamea had separated from Severus, let me now add a circumstance transmitted to us from our fathers, although it has not hitherto found a place in history. Cosmas, bishop of my native place, Epiphanea, which stands on the Orontes, and Severian, bishop of the neighboring city of Arethusa, being troubled at the synodical letters of Severus, and having withdrawn from his communion, despatched an instrument of deposition to him, while still bishop of Antioch. They entrust the document to

Aurelian, chief of the deacons at Epiphanea, and he, through dread of Severus and the majesty of so great a bishopric, on his arrival at Antioch puts on a female dress, and approaches Severus with delicate carriage and the entire assumption of a woman's appearance. Letting his veil fall down to his breast, with wailing and deep drawn lamentation he presents to Severus, as he advanced, the instruments of deposition in the guise of a petition: he then passes unobserved from among the attendant crowd and purchased safety by flight, before Severus had learned the purport of the document. Severus, having received the document and learned its contents, continued, nevertheless, in his see, until the death of Anastasius.

On being informed of these transactions, for I must record the benevolent measure of Anastasius, he directs Asiaticus, who was commander in Phœnicia Libanensis, to eject Cosmas and Severian from their sees, because they had sent the instrument of deposition to Severus. Finding, on his arrival in the East, that many adhered to the opinions of those bishops, and that their cities resolutely upheld them, he reported to Anastasius that he could not eject them without bloodshed. So great then was the humanity of Anastasius, that he wrote in express terms to Asiaticus, that he did not desire the accomplishment of any object, however important and illustrious, if one drop of blood was to be shed.

Such, then, was the situation of the churches throughout the world down to the reign of Anastasius; whom some, treating him as an enemy to the synod at Chalcedon, erased from the sacred diptychs; and he was also anathematized at Jerusalem even during his life-time.

CHAPTER XXXV

SUPPRESSION OF THE ISAURIAN INSURRECTION.

It will not be inconsistent, if, in accordance with the promise which I originally made, I insert in my narrative the other circumstances worthy of mention which occurred in the time of Anastasius.

Longinus, the kinsman of Zeno, on his arrival at his native country, as has been already detailed, openly commences war against the emperor: and after a numerous army had been raised from different quarters in which Conon, formerly bishop of Apamea in Syria was also present, who, as being an Isaurian, aided the Isaurians, an end was put to the war by the utter destruction of the Isaurian troops of Longinus. The heads of Longinus and Theodore were sent to the imperial city by John the Scythian; which the emperor displayed on poles at the place called Sycæ, opposite Constantinople, an agreeable spectacle to the Byzantines, who had been hardly treated by Zeno and the Isaurians. The other Longinus, surnamed of Selinus, the main stay of the insurgent faction, and Indes, are sent alive to Anastasius by John, surnamed Hunchback; a circumstance which especially gladdened the emperor and the Byzantines, by the display of the prisoners led in triumph along the streets and the hippodrome, with iron chains about their necks and hands. Thenceforward, also, the payment called Isaurica accrued to the imperial treasury, being gold previously paid to the Barbarians annually, to the amount of five thousand pounds.

Gold !

CHAPTER XXXVI

INVASION OF THE ARABS.

The Scenite barbarians also insulted the Roman empire; not, however, to their own advantage; by plundering Mesopotamia, either Phœnicia, and Palestine. After AD 500 having been everywhere chastised by the commanders, they subsequently continued quiet, and universally made peace with the Romans.

CHAPTER XXXVII

CAPTURE OF AMIDA. FOUNDING OF DARAS.

The Persians too, having, in violation of treaties, marched beyond their own territories under their king Cabades, first attacked Armenia, and having captured a town named Theodosiopolis, reached Amida, a strong city of Mesopotamia, which they took by storm; and which the Roman emperor subsequently restored by great exertions.

If any one is inclined to learn the particulars of these transactions, and to trace the whole minutely, a very able narrative, a work of great labor and elegance, has been composed by Eustathius; who, after having brought down his history to this point, was numbered with the departed; closing with the twelfth year of the reign of Anastasius.

After the close of this war, Anastasius founds a city on the spot called Daras in Mesopotamia, situated near the limits of the Roman dominion, and, as it were, a border-point of the two empires. He surrounds it with strong fortifications, and embellishes it with various stately erections, both of churches and other sacred buildings, basilicas, public baths, and other ornaments of distinguished cities. The place is said by some to have obtained the name of Daras, because there Alexander the Macedonian, the son of Philip, utterly defeated Darius.

CHAPTER XXXVIII

THE LONG WALL.

By the same emperor was raised a vast and memorable work called the Long Wall, in a favorable situation in Thrace, distant from Constantinople two hundred and eighty stadia. It reaches from one sea to the other, like a strait, to the extent of four hundred and twenty stadia; making the city an island, in a manner, instead of a peninsula, and affording a

AD 507

very safe transit, to such as choose, from the Pontus to the Euxine Sea. It is a check upon the inroads of the Barbarians from the Euxine, and of the Colchians from the Palus Mæotis, and from beyond the Caucasus, as well as of those who have made irruptions from Europe.

CHAPTER XXXIX

ABOLITION OF THE CHRYSARGYRUM.

The same emperor completed an extraordinary and divine achievement, namely, the entire abolition of the tax called chrysargyrum: which transaction I must now detail, though the task needs the eloquence of Thucydides, or something still more lofty and graceful. I will, however, myself describe it, not in reliance upon powers of language, but encouraged by the nature of the action.

There was imposed upon the Roman commonwealth, so singular in its magnitude and duration, a tax vile and hateful to God, and unworthy even of Barbarians, much more of the most Christian empire of the Romans: which, having been overlooked, from what cause I am unable to say, until the time of Anastasius, he most royally abolished. It was imposed, both on many other classes of persons who procured their livelihood by an accumulation of petty gains, and also upon women who made a sale of their charms, and surrendered themselves in brothels to promiscuous fornication in the obscure parts of the city; and besides, upon those who were devoted to a prostitution which outraged not only nature but the common weal: so that this mode of revenue proclaimed, as distinctly as a direct enactment, that all who chose, might practice such wickedness in security. The impious and accursed revenue raised from this source, the collectors paid at the end of every five years into the hands of the first and most dignified of the prefects: so that it formed no unimportant part of the functions of that office, and had its separate exchequer, and accountants, men who regarded the business as a military service, suited, like the rest, to persons of some distinction.

Anastasius, being informed of the circumstance, laid the matter before the senate, and justly declaring it to be an abomination and unparalleled defilement, decreed that it should be utterly abolished; and committed to the flames the papers which were vouchers for its collection. With the desire also of making this measure a complete sacrifice to God, and of preventing any of his successors from reviving the ancient shame, he puts on the appearance of vexation, and accuses himself of inconsiderateness and excessive folly, saying that in the too eager pursuit of novelty he had neglected the interests of the commonwealth, and had rashly and thoughtlessly abolished so important a revenue, which had been established in former times and confirmed by so long a continuance, without duly weighing the impending dangers, or the expenses necessary for the maintenance of the army, that living bulwark of the empire, nor yet for the service of God. Accordingly, without betraying his secret thoughts, he proclaims his desire to restore the before-mentioned revenue; and having summoned those who had been in charge of the levy, he told them that he repented of the step, but knew not what course to take, or how to rectify his error, now that the papers had been burnt which could be vouchers for the particulars of its exaction. And while they, on their part, lamented the abolition of the levy, not in semblance but in reality, on account of the unrighteous gain which had thence accrued to them, and were professing the same perplexity as the emperor, he urged and exhorted them to employ every mode of search, in the endeavor to procure from among documents preserved in various quarters, a statement of the entire levy. Supplying each individual with money, he despatched him to collect materials, enjoining him to bring every paper which threw light upon this matter wherever it might be found; that by means of the utmost circumspection and minute attention, a statement of the business might be again put together.

Accordingly, on the return of those who were engaged in the execution of these orders, Anastasius put on a pleased and gladsome appearance, and was in reality rejoiced in having compassed the object on which he was bent. He also made particular enquiries, both how they were discovered and in whose possession, and whether any thing of the same kind was still remaining: and on their affirming that they had expended great pains upon the collection, and swearing by the emperor himself, that no other paper which could be a voucher was preserved throughout the whole empire, Anastasius again lighted up a great pile with the papers thus produced, and drenched the ashes with water, with the intention of removing every trace of this levy; so that there might appear neither dust, nor ashes, nor any remnant whatever of the business, through imperfect combustion.

In order, however, that while we are thus extolling the abolition of this impost, we may not seem to be ignorant how much has been written under passionate feelings on the subject by former authors, let me produce these matters, and show their falsehood, and that more especially from their own statements.

CHAPTER XL
FALSEHOODS OF THE HISTORIAN ZOSIMUS.

Zosimus, a follower of the accursed and foul religion of the Greeks, in his anger against Constantine, because he was the first emperor that had adopted Christianity, abandoning the abominable superstition of the Greeks, says that he was the person who devised the tax called Chrysargyrum, and enacted that it should be levied every five years. He has on many other grounds also reviled that pious and magnificent monarch; for he affirms that he contrived many other intolerable proceedings against every class of persons; that he miserably destroyed his son Crispus, and made away with his wife Fausta by inclosing her in an overheated bath; and that after having in vain endeavored to procure purification from murders so detestable at the hands of the priests of his own religion (for they plainly declared its impossibility), he met with an Egyptian who had come from Iberia; and, having been assured by him that the faith of the Christians had the power of blotting out every sin, he embraced what the Egyptian had imparted to him, and thenceforward abandoning the faith of his fathers, he made the commencement of his impiety. The falsehood of these assertions I will forthwith show, and in the first place treat of the matter of the Chrysargyrum.

CHAPTER XLI

REFUTATION OF ZOSIMUS.

Thou sayest, O evil and malignant demon, that Constantine, wishing to raise a city equal to Rome, first made a commencement of so vast a place by laying strong foundations and erecting a lofty wall between Troas and Ilium; but when he had discovered in Byzantium a more suitable site, he in such fashion encircled the place with walls, so far extended the former city, and embellished it with buildings so splendid, as hardly to be surpassed by Rome itself, which had received gradual increase through so long a course of years. Thou sayest also that he made a distribution of provisions at the public cost to the people of Byzantium, and bestowed a very large sum of gold upon those who had accompanied him thither, for the erection of private houses.

Again, thou writest to the following effect: that on the decease of Constantine, the imperial power came into the hands of Constantius, his only surviving son after the death of his two brothers; and that when Magnentius and Vetranio had assumed the sovereignty, he wrought upon the latter by persuasives: and when both armies had been mustered, Constantius, addressing them first, reminded the soldiers of the generosity of his father, with whom they had served through many wars, and by whom they had been distinguished with the most liberal gifts; and that the soldiers, on hearing this, stripped Vetranio of his imperial robe, and made him descend from the tribunal into a private station; and that he suffered no unkindness at the hands of Constantius: who has shared with his father in so much of thy calumny. How thou canst then maintain that the same person could be so liberal, so munificent, and at the same time so paltry and sordid as to impose so accursed a tax, I am utterly unable to comprehend.

In proof that Constantine did not destroy Fausta or Crispus, nor was on that account initiated by an Egyptian into our mysteries, listen to the history of Eusebius Pamphili, who was contemporary with Constantine and Crispus, and had intercourse with them. For what thou writest, so far from being truth, was not even contemporary hearsay, since thou livedst long after, in the time of Arcadius and Honorius—to which period thou hast brought down thy history—or even after their time.

Eusebius, in the eighth book of his ecclesiastical history, has the following words: "After no very long interval, the emperor Constantine, having maintained a disposition remarkable for gentleness in respect to his whole life, kindliness towards his subjects, and favor towards the divine word, closes his life by the common laws of nature, leaving behind him, as emperor and Augustus in his own room, a legitimate son, Constantius." And farther on he says: "His son Constantius, having at the very commencement of his reign been proclaimed supreme emperor and Augustus by the armies, and long before by God himself, the universal Sovereign, showed himself an imitator of his father's piety as respects our faith." And at the end of the history he expresses himself in the following terms: "The mighty, victorious Constantine, distinguished by every religious excellence, in conjunction with his son Crispus, a sovereign highly beloved of God, and resembling his father in all things, obtained his rightful possession of the East."

Eusebius, who survived Constantine, would never have praised Crispus in these terms, if he had been destroyed by his father. Theodoret, in his history, says that Constantine partook in the saving baptism at Nicomedia, near the close of his life, and that he had deferred the rite till this period, from a desire that it should be performed in the river Jordan.

Thou sayest, O most detestable and polluted one, that the Roman empire from the time of the appearance of Christianity, fell away and was altogether ruined: either because thou hast not read any of the older writings, or because thou art a traitor to the truth. For, on the contrary, it clearly appears that the Roman power increased together with the spread of our faith. Consider, for instance, how, at the very time of the sojourn of Christ our God among mankind, the greater part of the Macedonians were crushed by the Romans, and Albania, Iberia, the Colchians, and Arabians were subjugated. Caius Cæsar also, in the hundred and eighty-first Olympiad, subdued in great battles the Gauls, Germans, and Britons, and thereby added to the Roman empire the inhabitants of five hundred cities; as has been recorded by historians. He also was the first who attained to sole sovereignty since the establishment of consuls, thereby preparing a way for the previous introduction of a reverence for monarchy, after the prevalence of polytheism and popular rule, on account of the monarchy of Christ which was immediately to appear.

A further acquisition was also forthwith made of the whole of Judæa and the neighboring territories: so that it was at this time that the first registration took place; in which Christ also was enrolled, in order that Bethlehem might fulfil the prophecy relating to it; for thus had the prophet Micah spoken respecting that place: "And thou, Bethlehem, territory of Judah, art by no means least among the princes of Judah, for from thee shall come forth a governor who shall feed my people Israel." Also after the nativity of Christ our God, Egypt was added to the Roman dominion; Augustus Cæsar, in whose time Christ was born, having completely overthrown Antony and Cleopatra; who also killed themselves. Upon which Cornelius Gallus is appointed by Augustus governor of Egypt, being the first who ruled that country after the Ptolemies: as has been recorded by historians. To what extent the territories of the Persians were curtailed by Ventidius, Corbulo the general of Nero, Severus, Trajan, Carus, Cassius, Odenatus of Palmyra, Apollonius, and others; and how often Seleucia and Ctesiphon were taken, and Nisibis changed sides; and how Armenia and the neighboring countries were added to the Roman empire; these matters have been narrated by thyself, as well as by others.

I had, however, nearly forgotten to notice what thou thyself writest respecting the achievements of Constantine, how nobly and courageously he swayed the Roman empire, while professing our religion, and what befell Julian, thy hero and the votary of thy orgies, who bequeathed to the commonwealth injuries so serious. Whether, however, he has either already received a foretaste of the things which have been foretold concerning the end of the world, or will even receive their full measure, is a question relating to an economy too high for thy comprehension.

Let us, at all events, consider under what circumstances heathen and Christian emperors have respectively closed their reigns. Did not Caius Julius Cæsar, the first sole sovereign, close his life by assassination? In the next place, did not some of his own officers dispatch with their swords Caius, the grandson of Tiberius? Was not Nero slain by one of his domestics? Did not Galba, Otho, and Vitellius, who reigned in all only sixteen months, suffer a similar fate? Was not Titus, on his attaining the empire, taken off by poison by his own brother Domitian? Was not Domitian himself miserably despatched by Stephanus? What too dost thou say about Commodus? Was not he killed by

Narcissus? Pertinax and Julian, did they not meet with the same treatment? Antoninus, the son of Severus, did he not murder his brother Geta, and was himself murdered by Martial? Macrinus too, was he not dragged about Byzantium, like a captive, and then butchered by his own soldiers? And Aurelius Antoninus, the Emesene, was he not slaughtered together with his mother? And his successor Alexander, was he not, together with his mother, involved in a similar catastrophe? What should I say, too, concerning Maximin, who was slain by his own troops? Or Gordian, brought to a similar end by the designs of Philip? Tell me whether Philip and his successor Decius did not perish by the hands of their enemies? And Gallus and Volusian by their own armies? Æmilian, was he not involved in the same fate? And Valerian, was he not made prisoner and carried about as a show by the Persians?

After the assassination of Gallienus and the murder of Carinus, the sovereignty came into the hands of Diocletian and those whom he chose as his partners in the empire. Of these, Herculius, Maximian, and Maxentius his son, and Licinius utterly perished. But from the time that the renowned Constantine succeeded to the empire, and had dedicated to Christ the city which bears his name, mark me, whether any of those who have reigned there, except Julian thy hierophant and monarch, have perished by the hands of either domestic or foreign foes, and whether a rival has overthrown any of them; except that Basiliscus expelled Zeno, by whom, however, he was afterwards overthrown and killed. I also agree with thee in what thou sayest about Valens, who had inflicted so many evils upon the Christians: for of any other case not even thou thyself makest mention.

Let no one think that these matters are foreign to an ecclesiastical history; since they are, in fact, altogether useful and essential, on account of willful desertion of the cause of truth on the part of heathen writers. Let me now proceed to the rest of the acts of Anastasius.

CHAPTER XLII

THE GOLD-RATE.

The before-mentioned measures Anastasius successfully carried out in a truly royal spirit; but he adopted others by no means worthy of them: both by devising what is called the gold-rate, and farming out the supplies for the army on terms most burdensome to the provincials. He also took the levying of imposts out of the hands of the councils of the respective cities, and appointed what are called Vindices, at the suggestion, as is said, of Marinus the Syrian, who held the highest prefecture, termed in former times the Prefect of the Prætorium. The result was that the revenue fell off to a great extent, and the local dignitaries sunk into abeyance: for persons of high families formerly had their names inscribed in the album of each city; which regarded those who were members of its council, as a kind of senate.

CHAPTER XLIII

INSURRECTION OF VITALIAN.

Vitalian, a Thracian by birth, disputes the empire with Anastasius, and having devastated Thrace and Mysia as far as Odessus and Anchialus, was advancing rapidly upon the imperial city, at the head of an innumerable force of Huns. The emperor despatched Hypatius to encounter this force; and, after he had been captured through the treachery of his own troops, and liberated at a large ransom, the conduct of the war was entrusted to Cyril.

AD 514

The battle which followed was at first indecisive, with several subsequent alternations of success; but, notwithstanding the advantage was on the side of Cyril, the enemy rallied, and he was ultimately routed through the willful desertion of his own soldiers. In consequence,

Vitalian captured Cyril in Odessus, and advanced as far as the place called Sycæ, laying the whole country waste with fire and sword; meditating nothing less than the capture of the city itself and the seizure of the sovereignty. When he had encamped at Sycæ, Marinus the Syrian, whom we have mentioned before, is despatched by the emperor to attack him by sea. The two armaments, accordingly, encountered, the one having Sycæ astern, the other Constantinople. For a time the fleets remained inactive: but, after the skirmishings and discharge of missiles had been followed by a fierce conflict in the place called Bytharia, Vitalian withdraws from the line of battle and takes to flight with the loss of the greater portion of his fleet.[3] The remainder then fly with such precipitation, that the next day not a single enemy was found in the channel or in the neighborhood of the city. It is said that Vitalian then continued inactive for some time at Anchialus.

There was also another inroad of Huns, who had passed the defiles of Cappadocia.

About the same time Rhodes suffered by a violent earthquake at the dead of night: this being the third time it had been visited by that calamity.

CHAPTER XLIV

SEDITION AT CONSTANTINOPLE.

A very great sedition occurred at Byzantium, arising from a wish of the emperor to add to the Trisagion the clause, "Who was crucified for our sakes:" which was regarded as subversive of the Christian religion.[4] Its prime mover and chief was Macedonius, aided by his subject clergy, as Severus says in a letter to Sotericus, which he wrote before his elevation to the episcopal throne, while residing at the imperial city, at the time when, with several others, he had been expelled from his monastery, as I have already mentioned. It was on account of this imputation, in addition to

AD 518

the causes before mentioned, that, in my opinion, Macedonius was ejected from his see. Amid the uncontrollable excitement of the populace which followed, persons of rank and station were brought into extreme danger, and many principal parts of the city were set on fire. The populace, having found in the house of Marinus the Syrian, a monk from the country, cut off his head, saying that the clause had been added at his instigation and having fixed it upon a pole, jeeringly exclaimed: "See the plotter against the Trinity!"

Such was the violence of the tumult, filling every quarter with devastation, and surpassing every means of control, that the emperor was driven to appear at the Hippodrome in pitiable guise, without his crown, and despatched heralds to proclaim to the assembled people, that he was most ready to resign his sovereignty; at the same time reminding them, that it was impossible that all should be elevated to that dignity, which admitted not of a plurality of occupants, and that one individual only could be his successor.

At this the temper of the people was suddenly changed, as by some divine impulse; and they begged Anastasius to resume his crown; with a promise of peaceable conduct in future.

Anastasius survived this event a very short time, and departed to the other world after a reign of twenty-seven years, three months, and three days.

NOTES

1. Evagrius uses the term "Scenite barbarians" for the Arabs, who by the mid-5th century AD, were becoming a serious menace to both the Romans and Persians.

2. Whitby (p. 161) translates this term "Opportunity" while Chestnut has it as "the Opportune Moment." In Greek, the term is Kairos (Καιρος). For an interesting discussion of this amusing moralizing digression, see Chestnut, pp. 219–222.

3. According to the Chronicle of John Malalas, the forces of Anastasius were victorious in this battle thanks to the first recorded use of the substance known as Greek Fire (Bury, History of the Later Roman Empire, Vol. 1, pp. 451–452).

4. The Trisagion or "Thrice Holy" is a prayer in Greek that translates, "Holy God, Holy Mighty One, Holy Immortal One, have mercy on us." The insertion of

the phrase, "who was crucified for our sakes" is considered heretical because it insinuates that all the Persons of the Trinity suffered on the cross, not just God the Son. While Evagrius attributes this novelty to the Emperor Anastasius, it originated with Peter the Fuller, Patriarch of Antioch, some 40 years before this incident (Catholic Encyclopedia, Vol. 5, "Eutychianism").

THE FOURTH BOOK

CHAPTER I

ACCESSION OF JUSTIN.

After Anastasius had, as I have said, departed for the better lot, Justin, a Thracian by birth, assumes the purple, in the five hundred and sixty-sixth year of the Era of Antioch, on the ninth day of the month Panemus, which the Romans call July. He was proclaimed emperor by the Imperial body-guards, of which he was also the commander, having been appointed prefect of the household troops. His elevation was, however, contrary to all expectation, since there were many most distinguished and flourishing members of the family of Anastasius, possessed also of sufficient influence to have secured for themselves the supreme power.

CHAPTER II

DESIGNS AND DEATH OF AMANTIUS AND THEOCRITUS.

Amantius was the imperial chamberlain, and a man of very great influence; but as it was not lawful for any emasculated person to attain the sovereignty of the Romans, he was desirous that the imperial crown should be given to Theocritus, one of his creatures. He, therefore, sends for Justin, and gives him a large sum of money, with orders to distribute it amongst the persons most fit for this purpose, and able to invest Theocritus with the purple. But with the money he either bought over the people, or purchased the goodwill of what are termed the Excubitores—for both accounts are given—and so attained the empire. Soon afterwards he took off Amantius and Theocritus, with some others.

CHAPTER III

ASSASSINATION OF VITALIAN.

Justin sends for Vitalian, who was living in Thrace and who had entertained designs of dethroning Anastasius, to Constantinople: for he dreaded his power, his military experience, his universal renown, and his great desire to possess the sovereignty: and rightly conjecturing that he should not be able to overcome him otherwise than by pretending to be a friend. By way of concealing his guile under a plausible mask, he appoints him commander of one of the bodies called Præsentes, and, as a more effectual persuasive, with a view to a still greater deception, he raises him to the consulship. He, being consul elect, was assassinated on visiting the palace, at an inner door, and thus met with a punishment for his insolence towards the Roman sovereignty. But these events happened subsequently.

CHAPTER IV

DEPOSITION OF SEVERUS, BISHOP OF ANTIOCH. SUCCESSION OF PAUL AND EUPHRASIUS.

Severus, who had been ordained president of Antioch, as stated above, ceased not daily to anathematize the synod at Chalcedon, and chiefly by means of those epistles called

Book IV

Enthronistic, and in the respo   to all the
patriarchs; though they were rec   dria, by
John, the successor of the former .   is and
Timotheus: which epistles have co

Many contentions having thus   ch,
whereby the most faithful people w   s,
Justin, in the first year of his reign, orde   ,
and to be punished, as some say, by h
out; the execution of which sentence
Irenæus, who, at Antioch, held the governn
provinces.

Severus himself confirms the account o   ing
appointed to arrest him, in a letter to some of th Antiochenes,
describing the manner of his escape; wherein he casts the
strongest invectives on Irenæus, and states that he is under
the strictest surveillance lest he should escape from Antioch.
Some say that Vitalian, who still appeared to be in the highest
favor with Justin, demanded the tongue of Severus because he
had reproached him in his discourses.

Accordingly, he flies from his see, in the month
Gorpiæus, which in the Latin language is called September,
in the five hundred and sixty-seventh year of the Era
of Antioch. Paul succeeds to the see, with orders to   AD 519
proclaim openly the synod at Chalcedon. Afterwards, retiring
voluntarily from Antioch, he went the way of all flesh by a
natural death. He is succeeded in his see by Euphrasius from
Jerusalem.

CHAPTER V

FIRES AND EARTHQUAKES AT ANTIOCH.
DEATH OF EUPHRASIUS.

About the same period of Justin's reign there happened at
Antioch numerous and dreadful fires, as if harbingers of the
terrible shocks which afterwards took place, and serving as a

prelude for the coming calamities. For, a short time after, in the tenth month of the seventh year of Justin's reign, being Artemisius or May, on the twenty-ninth day of the month, precisely at noon, on the sixth day of the week, the city was visited with the shock of an earthquake, which very nearly destroyed the whole of it. This was followed by a fire, to share, as it were, in the calamity: for what escaped the earthquake, the fire in its spread reduced to ashes. The damage that the city sustained, how many persons according to probable estimate became the victims of the fire and earthquake, what strange occurrences surpassing the power of words took place, have been feelingly related by John the Rhetorician, who concludes his history with the relation.

AD 526

Euphrasius also perished in the ruins, to add another misfortune to the city, by leaving no one to provide for its exigencies.

CHAPTER VI

ELEVATION OF EPHRAEMIUS, COUNT OF THE EAST, TO THE PATRIARCHATE OF ANTIOCH.

But the saving care of God for man, which prepares the remedy before the stroke, and the compassion which, while sharpening the sword of wrath, at the moment of the deepest despair displays its sympathy, raised up Ephraemius, at that time governor of the Eastern provinces, to take upon himself all the care of the city; so that it lacked not any thing that its exigency required. On this account, the sons of the Antiochenes so admired him, that they elected him their priest: and he thus attains the apostolic see as a reward and prize of his singular care for the place. Thirty months after, the city suffered again from an earthquake.

At this time also, what had been hitherto called the city of Antiochus was entitled the City of God, and received additional care at the hands of the emperor.

CHAPTER VII

MIRACLES OF ZOSIMAS AND JOHN.

Now that I have recorded the above-mentioned calamities, let me also add to the present narrative some other circumstances worthy of record, and which have been transmitted to us from those who have made them a subject of notice.

Zosimas was a native of Sinde, a village of Phœnicia Maritima, distant from Tyre about twenty stadia, and pursued the monastic discipline. He, by means both of abstinence and use of food, having attained to such a union with God as not only to discern forthcoming events, but also to possess the grace of perfect freedom from passion, was in company with a distinguished person from Cæsarea, the capital of one of the Palestines. This was Arcesilaus, a man of good family, accomplished, and high in dignities and whatever gives lustre to life. Zosimas, at the very moment of the overthrow of Antioch, suddenly became troubled, uttered lamentations and deep sighs, and then shedding such a profusion of tears as to bedew the ground, called for a censer, and having fumed the whole place where they were standing, throws himself upon the ground, propitiating God with prayers and supplications. Upon Arcesilaus asking the reason of all this trouble, he distinctly replied, that the sound of the overthrow of Antioch was at that instant ringing in his ears. This led Arcesilaus and the rest of the astonished company to note down the hour; and they afterwards found that it was as Zosimas had said.

By his hand many other miracles were performed: but omitting the greater part of them, since they are too numerous to detail, I shall mention a few.

Contemporary with Zosimas, and endued with equal virtues, was a man named John, who had practiced the endurance of the solitary and immaterial life in the cloister called Chuzibas, situated at the extremity of the glen at the northern part of the highway leading from Jerusalem to Jericho, and was now bishop of the before-named Cæsarea. This John, the Chuzibite, having heard that the wife of Arcesilaus had lost one of her eyes by a stroke of a spindle, runs immediately to her to see the accident; and when he finds that, the pupil is gone and the eye altogether lacerated, he commands one of the physicians in attendance to bring a sponge, and, having replaced as well as he could the lacerated parts, to apply and secure the sponge with bandages. Arcesilaus was absent, for he happened to be with Zosimas in his monastery at Sinde, distant from Cæsarea a full five hundred stadia. Accordingly, messengers proceeded with all haste to Arcesilaus, whom they found sitting in conversation with Zosimas. When informed of the circumstance, he uttered a piercing cry, tore his hair and cast it towards heaven. Upon Zosimas asking him the reason, he told him what had happened, interrupting his account with frequent wailings and tears. Whereupon Zosimas, leaving him alone, goes to his chamber, where he used to make his addresses to God according to the rule of such persons, and after some interval he approaches Arcesilaus with a solemnly joyous countenance, and gently pressing his hand, said: "Depart with joy, depart. Grace is given to the Chuzibite. Your wife is cured, and is in possession of both her eyes; for the accident has had no power to deprive her of them, since such was the desire of the Chuzibite." This was brought about by the united wonder-working of both the just men.

Again, as the same Zosimas was going to Cæsarea, and leading an ass laden with certain necessaries, a lion encountered him and carried off the ass. Zosimas follows into the wood, reaches the place where the lion was, satiated with his meal upon the beast, and smiling says, "Come, my friend; my journey is interrupted, since I am heavy and far advanced in years, and not able to carry on my back the ass's load. You must therefore carry it, though contrary to your nature, if you wish Zosimas to get out of this place and yourself to be a wild beast again." All at once the lion, forgetting his ferocity, fawned on him, and by his gestures plainly manifested obedience. Zosimas then put the ass's load upon him, and led him to the gates of Cæsarea, showing the power of God, and how all things are subservient to man if we live to Him and do not pervert the grace given to us. But that I may not render my history prolix by more circumstances of the kind, I will return to the point whence I digressed.

CHAPTER VIII
GENERAL CALAMITIES.

During the reign of Justin, Dyrrachium, formerly called Epidamnus, suffered from an earthquake; as did also Corinth in Greece, and afterwards, for the fourth time, Anazarbus, the capital of Cilicia Minor. These cities Justin restored at great expense. About the same time Edessa, a large and flourishing city of Osroene, was inundated by the waters of the Skirtus, which runs close by it; so that most of the buildings were swept away, and countless multitudes that were carried down by the stream, perished. Accordingly, the names of Edessa and Anazarbus were changed by Justin, and each of them was called, after himself, Justinopolis.

AD 525

CHAPTER IX
APPOINTMENT OF JUSTINIAN
TO A SHARE IN THE EMPIRE.

When Justin had reigned eight years, nine months, and three days, he associated in the government Justinian, his nephew, who was proclaimed on the first of the month Xanthicus, or April, in the five hundred and seventy-fifth year of the era of Antioch. After these transactions, Justin departs his earthly sovereignty, closing his life on the first of the month Lous, or August, having had Justinian[1] for his associate in the

AD 527

empire four months, and reigned in all nine years and three days. Now that Justinian was sole sovereign of the Roman empire, and the synod at Chalcedon was being proclaimed in the most holy churches by the commands of Justin, as stated before; the state of the church was disturbed in some of the provinces, but chiefly at Constantinople and Alexandria, Anthimus being bishop of the former, and Theodosius of the latter: for both held the doctrine of the single nature of Christ.

CHAPTER X

THE COUNCIL OF CHALCEDON UPHELD BY JUSTINIAN.

Justinian very resolutely upheld the synod at Chalcedon and what was put forth by it; and Theodora, his consort, those who maintained the single nature: either because such were their real sentiments—for when the faith is a matter of dispute, fathers are divided against their children, children against the authors of their birth, a wife against her own husband, and again a husband against his own wife—or by mutual understanding, that he should uphold those who maintained the two natures in Christ our God after the union; and she those who alleged the single nature. Neither conceded to the other: but he strenuously supported the acts at Chalcedon, and she, ranging with the opposite party, exercised the greatest care towards those who maintained the single nature. Our people she treated with the warmest kindness, and others too with great munificence. She also persuades Justinian to send for Severus.

CHAPTER XI

DEPOSITION OF ANTHIMUS AND THEODOSIUS FROM THEIR SEES.

There are letters extant from Severus to Justinian and Theodora, from which we may gather that at first he put off his journey to the imperial city on leaving his see of Antioch. Nevertheless he afterwards arrived there; and has written to the effect that when he came thither and had conversed with Anthimus, and found him holding the same sentiments with himself, and the same opinions with respect to the Godhead, he persuaded him to withdraw from his see. He wrote concerning these matters to Theodosius, bishop of Alexandria, and greatly gloried in having persuaded Anthimus, as stated before, to prefer such doctrines to earthly glory and the possession of his see.

Letters are also extant on this subject from Anthimus to Theodosius, and from Theodosius to Severus and Anthimus; which I pass over, leaving them to those who choose to consult them, that I may not include in the present work too great a mass of materials. Nevertheless, both were ejected from their sees, as opposing the imperial mandates and the decrees of Chalcedon. Zoilus succeeded to that of Alexandria, and Epiphanius to that of the imperial city: so that from that time forward the synod at Chalcedon was openly proclaimed in all the churches; and no one dared to anathematize it; while those who dissented, were urged by innumerable methods to assent to it. Accordingly, a constitution was drawn up by Justinian in which, he anathematized Severus, Anthimus, and others, and subjected those who held their doctrines, to the highest penalties: the effect of which was, that thenceforward no schism remained in any of the churches, but the patriarchs of the several dioceses agreed with each other, and the bishops of the cities followed their respective primates.

Four synods were thus proclaimed throughout the churches; first, that held at Nicæa; secondly, that at Constantinople; thirdly, the former one at Ephesus; and fourthly, that at Chalcedon. A fifth also took place by order of Justinian, concerning which I shall say what is suitable in its proper place, while I weave into my present narrative the several events of the same period which are worthy of notice.

CHAPTER XII

CABADES AND CHOSROES, KINGS OF PERSIA.

The history of Belisarius has been written by Procopius the Rhetorician. He says that Cabades, king of the Persians, wishing to invest his youngest son Chosroes with the sovereignty, was desirous to have him adopted by the Roman emperor, so that by that means his succession might be secured. But when this was refused, at the suggestion of Proclus, who advised Justinian as his quæstor, they conceived a still greater hatred against the Romans. The same Procopius has, with diligence, elegance, and ability, set forth the events of the war between the Romans and Persians while Belisarius was commander of the forces of the East. The first victory on the side of the Romans which he records, was in the neighborhood of Daras and Nisibis, under the command of Belisarius and Hermogenes.

AD 531

He subjoins an account of the occurrences in Armenia, and the mischief inflicted on the Romans by Alamundarus, the chieftain of the Scenite barbarians, who captured Timostratus, the brother of Rufinus, together with his troops, and afterwards liberated him for a considerable ransom.

CHAPTER XIII

INCURSION OF THE ARABS.
SEDITION AT CONSTANTINOPLE.

He also feelingly details the incursion of the before-mentioned Alamundarus and Azarethus into the Roman territory; and how Belisarius, compelled by his own troops, engaged them in their retreat by the Euphrates, on the eve of Easter day; and how the Roman army was destroyed through their repugnance to the measures of Belisarius; and how Rufinus and Hermogenes made with the Persians the peace called the perpetual peace.

He subjoins an account of the insurrection of the people at Byzantium, which derived its name from the watchword of the populace: for they entitled it "Nika"[2], because on their assembling they chose this term as the watchword, to know each other. On this occasion Hypatius and Pompeius were compelled by the people to assume the sovereignty. But on the defeat of the populace, both were beheaded by the soldiers at the command of Justinian, and the insurrection was quelled. Procopius states that thirty thousand persons were killed in this disturbance.

CHAPTER XIV

PERSECUTION BY HUNERIC.

The same writer, when treating of the affairs of the Vandals, has recorded most important occurrences and worthy of perpetual memory, which I now proceed to mention. Huneric, the successor of Genseric, and a professor of the creed of Arius, entertained most cruel intentions against the African Christians, in the endeavor to convert by force the maintainers of the orthodox doctrines to the opinions of the Arians. Those who refused compliance, he destroyed both by fire and various modes of death, and some he deprived of their tongues. The latter, Procopius says that he himself saw, when they had taken refuge at the imperial city, and that he maintained a conversation with them in the same manner as with unmutilated persons: that their tongues were cut out from the root; nevertheless their speech was articulate, and they conversed distinctly; a new and strange marvel, of which also a constitution of Justinian makes mention. Two of these persons lapsed, as Procopius himself writes. For on their desiring commerce with women, they were deprived of their speech, since the grace of their martyrdom had abandoned them.

CHAPTER XV

CABAONES THE MOOR.

He also relates another wonderful occurrence, wrought by our Savior God in the case of men, aliens indeed to our religion, who, however, acted with religious reverence. He states that Cabaones was chieftain of the Moors in the neighborhood of Tripolis. This Cabaones, he says—for it is worth while to use his own words during his able narration of this matter also—this Cabaones, as soon as he learned that the Vandals were marching against him, acted in the following manner. First, he commanded all his subjects to refrain from injustice and all luxurious food, but particularly from commerce with women; and having raised two fortified enclosures, he encamped himself with all the men in one, and enclosed the women in the other, threatening death to any man who should approach the women. Afterwards, he sent scouts to Carthage with these instructions: that when the Vandals on their march outraged any temple reverenced by the Christians, they should note what was being done, and when the Vandals left the place, should, immediately on their departure, treat the sanctuary in a manner directly the reverse. It is mentioned that he further said, that he was ignorant of the God worshipped by the Christians, but it was likely, if he were powerful, as was affirmed, that he would chastise those who outraged him, and defend such as rendered him service. The scouts, therefore, coming to Carthage, continued to watch the preparations of the Vandals, and when the army set forward for Tripolis, they followed it, disguised in a sorry dress.

The Vandals, encamping at the close of the first day, introduced their horses and other beasts into the temples of the Christians, and abstained from no species of outrage, but gave way to their usual license; and beating and severely scourging the priests whom they happened to seize, bid

AD 522

them wait upon them. But as soon as the Vandals had left the place, the scouts of Cabaones did all that had been enjoined them, and immediately cleansed the sanctuaries, sedulously removing the dung and every other defilement: they lighted all the tapers, paid reverent obeisance to the priests, and saluted them with every kindness; and when they had bestowed money on the beggars who sat round the shrine, they followed the army of the Vandals, who, from this point along the whole line of march, committed the same outrages, while the scouts remedied them. When, however, they were at no great distance, the scouts, proceeding in advance, announced to Cabaones all that had been done by the Vandals and themselves to the temples of the Christians, and that, the enemy were now near. On hearing this, he prepared to engage.

By far the greater part of the Vandals, as our author states, were destroyed: some were captured by the enemy, and very few returned home. Such was the misfortune that Thrasamund sustained at the hands of the Moors. He died some time after, having ruled the Vandals for seven and twenty years.

CHAPTER XVI

EXPEDITION OF BELISARIUS AGAINST THE VANDALS.

The same author writes that Justinian, having, in pity to the Christians in that quarter, professed his intention of undertaking an expedition for their relief, was being diverted from his purpose by the suggestion of John, prefect of the palace,[3] when a dream appeared to him, bidding him not to shrink from the execution of his design; for, by assisting the Christians he would overthrow the power of the Vandals. Being determined by this circumstance, in the seventh year of his reign, he despatches Belisarius, about the summer solstice, to attack Carthage; on which occasion, when the general's ship touched at the shore of the palace, Epiphanius, bishop of the city, offered up appropriate prayers, having previously baptized some of the soldiers and embarked them on board the vessel. He also narrates some circumstances, worthy of record, relating to the martyr Cyprian, in the following words:

"All the Carthaginians especially reverence Cyprian, a holy man, and having erected on the shore, in front of their city, a noble shrine, besides other reverential observances, they celebrate an annual festival, and call it Cypriana; and the sailors are accustomed to call the tempestuous weather which I have before mentioned by the same name as the festival, since it is wont to happen at the time of the year at which the Africans have fixed its perpetual celebration. This temple the Vandals, in the reign of Huneric, took by force from the Christians, and ignominiously expelling the priests, refitted it, as henceforward belonging to the Arians. They say that Cyprian, frequently appearing in a dream to the Africans who were indignant and distressed on this account, told them that there was occasion for the Christians to be solicitous about him, for in time he would avenge himself: which prediction attained its accomplishment in the time of Belisarius, when Carthage, ninety-five years after its loss, was reduced by him under the Roman power, by the utter overthrow of the Vandals: at which time the doctrine of the Arians was entirely extirpated from Africa, and the Christians recovered their own temples, according to the prediction of the martyr Cyprian."

AD 533

CHAPTER XVII

TRIUMPH OF BELISARIUS.

The same author writes as follows: "When Belisarius had subdued the Vandals, he returned to Byzantium, bringing the spoils and prisoners, and among them Gelimer, king of the Vandals. A triumph was granted him, and he carried in procession through the Hippodrome whatever would be an object of wonder. Among these were considerable treasures obtained by Genseric from the plunder of the palace at Rome, as I have already narrated; when Eudoxia, the wife of Valentinian, emperor of the West, having been both deprived of her husband and subjected to an outrage on her chastity by Maximus, invited Genseric, with a promise of surrendering the city to him: on which occasion, after burning Rome, he conveyed Eudoxia and her daughters to the country of the Vandals. Together with the other treasures, he then carried off all that Titus, the son of Vespasian, had brought to Rome on the capture of Jerusalem; offerings which Solomon had dedicated to God. These Justinian, in honor of Christ our God, sent back to Jerusalem; an act of becoming reverence to the Deity, to whom they had in the first instance been dedicated.

On this occasion, Procopius says that Gelimer, prostrating himself on the ground in the hippodrome, before the imperial throne on which Justinian was sitting to witness the proceedings, made application, in his own language, of the divine oracle: "Vanity of vanities; all is vanity."

CHAPTER XVIII

ORIGIN OF THE MOORS. MUNIFICENCE OF JUSTINIAN IN AFRICA.

Procopius mentions another circumstance, unnoticed before his time, but one that can scarcely be regarded with sufficient wonder. He states that the Moors of Lybia settled in that country after being dislodged from Palestine, and that they are those whom the divine oracles mention as the Girgashites and Jebusites, and the other nations subdued by Joshua the son of Nun. He concludes the entire truth of the story from an inscription in Phœnician characters, which he says that he himself had read, and that it was near a fountain, where were two pillars of white stone on which were engraved these words: "We are those who fled from the face of Joshua the robber, the son of Nun." Such was the end of these transactions, Africa becoming again subject to the Romans, and paying, as before, an annual tribute.

Justinian is said to have restored one hundred and fifty cities in Africa, some of which had been altogether, and others extensively ruined; and this he did with surpassing magnificence, in private and public works and embellishments, in fortifications, and other vast structures by which cities are adorned and the Deity propitiated: also in aqueducts for use and ornament, the supply of water having been in some cases conveyed to the cities for the first time, in others restored to its former state.

CHAPTER XIX

EVENTS FOLLOWING THE DEATH OF THEODORIC.

I now proceed to relate what occurred in Italy; events which have also been treated very distinctly by Procopius the Rhetorician, down to his own times.

After Theodoric, as I have already detailed, had captured Rome and utterly destroyed its king Odoacer, and had closed his life in possession of the Roman sovereignty, his wife Amalasuntha held the reins of government, as guardian of their common son Athalaric; a woman rather of a masculine temperament, and administering affairs accordingly.[4] She was the first person who led Justinian to entertain a desire for the Gothic war, by sending an embassy to him on the formation of a conspiracy against herself. On the death, however, of Athalaric at a very early age, Theodatus, a kinsman of Theodoric, was invested with the sovereignty of the West, but abdicated when Justinian had despatched Belisarius to that quarter; being a person addicted rather to literature, and altogether wanting in military experience; while Vitiges, an able soldier, was in command of his forces.

From the materials which the same Procopius has collected, one may gather that Vitiges abandoned Rome on the arrival of Belisarius in Italy; who at once marched upon the city. The Romans readily opened their gates to him; a result mainly brought about by Silverius, their bishop, who with this view, had sent to him Fidelis, formerly assessor to Athalaric. They accordingly surrendered their city to him without resistance: and thus Rome, after an interval of sixty years, again fell into Roman hands on the ninth day of the month Apellæus, called by the Latins December. The same Procopius writes, that, when the Goths were besieging Rome, Belisarius, suspecting Silverius of a design to betray the city, transports him to Greece and appoints Vigilius in his room.

AD 536

CHAPTER XX

CONVERSION OF THE HERULI.

About the same time, as Procopius also writes, when the Heruli, who had already crossed the river Danube in the reign of Anastasius, had experienced generous treatment at the hands of Justinian, in large presents of money, the whole nation embraced Christianity and adopted a more civilized mode of life.

CHAPTER XXI

LOSS AND RECOVERY OF ROME.

In the next place he records the return of Belisarius to Byzantium, and how he brought thither Vitiges, together with the spoils of Rome; also the seizure of the sovereignty of Rome by Totila, and how the city again fell under the dominion of a Goth; how Belisarius, having twice entered Italy, again recovered the city, and how, on the breaking out of the Median war, he was recalled to Byzantium by the emperor.

CHAPTER XXII
CONVERSION OF THE ABASGI.

Procopius also records that the Abasgi, having become more civilized, embraced the Christian doctrine about the same time, and that Justinian sent to them one of the eunuchs of the palace, their countryman, by name Euphratas, with an interdict, that henceforward no one in that nation should undergo emasculation in violation of nature; for from among them the imperial chamberlains were principally appointed, whom usage styles eunuchs. At this time, Justinian, having erected among the Abasgi a temple in honor of the Mother of God, appointed priests for them; by which means they were accurately instructed in the Christian doctrine.

CHAPTER XXIII
CONVERSION OF THE PEOPLE ON THE TANAIS. EARTHQUAKES.

The same author narrates, that the people on the Tanais (the natives give the name of Tanais to the channel extending from the Palus Mæotis to the Euxine Sea) urged Justinian to send a bishop to them; which request he granted, and gladly sent them a priest. The same writer describes, with great ability, the irruptions of the Goths of the Mæotis into the Roman territory in the time of Justinian, and the violent earthquakes which took place in Greece; how Bœotia, Achaia and the neighborhood of the Crissæan bay suffered shocks; how innumerable towns and cities were levelled, and chasms were formed, many of which closed again, while others remained open.

CHAPTER XXIV
ACHIEVEMENTS AND PIETY OF NARSES.

Procopius also describes the expedition of Narses, who was sent by Justinian into Italy; how he overthrew Totila and afterwards Teia; and how Rome was taken for the fifth time. Those about the person of Narses affirm that he used to propitiate the Deity with prayers and other acts of piety, paying due honor also to the Virgin and mother of God, so that she distinctly announced to him the proper season for action; and that Narses never engaged until he had received the signal from her. He recounts also other distinguished exploits of Narses in the overthrow of Buselinus and Syndualdus, and the acquisition of nearly the whole country as far as the ocean. These transactions have been recounted by Agathias the Rhetorician, but his history has not reached our hands.

CHAPTER XXV
INVASION OF THE PERSIANS.
CAPTURE OF ANTIOCH.

The same Procopius has also written the following account. When Chosroes had learned what had occurred in Africa and Italy favorable to the Roman dominion, he was moved to excessive jealousy, and advanced certain charges against the Roman government, that terms had been violated and the existing peace broken. In the first place, Justinian sent ambassadors to Chosroes to induce him not to break the peace which was intended to be perpetual, nor to trespass on the existing conditions; proposing that the points in dispute should be discussed and settled in an amicable manner. But AD 540 Chosroes, maddened by the ferment of jealousy, would not listen to any proposals, and invaded the Roman territory with a large army, in the thirteenth year of the reign of Justinian.

The historian also writes, that Chosroes captured and destroyed Sura, a city on the banks of the Euphrates, after having professed to make terms, but dealing with it in defiance of all justice, by paying no regard to the conditions, and becoming master of it rather by stratagem than by open war. He also narrates the burning of Beræa, and then the advance upon Antioch; at which time Ephraemius was the bishop of the city, but had abandoned it on the failure of all his plans. This person is said to have rescued the church and its precincts, by arraying it with the sacred offerings, in order that they might serve as a ransom for it.

The historian also feelingly describes the capture of Antioch by Chosroes, and its promiscuous devastation by fire and sword: his visit to the neighboring city of Seleucia, and to the suburb Daphne, and his advance toward Apamea, during the episcopate of Thomas, a man most powerful in word and deed. He had the prudence to yield to Chosroes in becoming a spectator of the horse-races in the hippodrome, though an act of irregularity; employing every means to court and pacify the conqueror. Chosroes also asked him whether he was desirous to see him in his own city: and it is said that he frankly replied that it was no pleasure to see him in his neighborhood: at which answer Chosroes was struck with wonder, justly admiring the truthfulness of the man.

CHAPTER XXVI

DISPLAY OF THE WOOD OF THE CROSS AT APAMEA.

Now that I have arrived at this point of my narrative, I will relate a prodigy, which occurred at Apamea, and is worthy of a place in the present history.

When the sons of the Apameans were informed that Antioch had been burnt, they besought the before-mentioned Thomas to bring forth and display the saving and life-giving wood of the cross, in deviation from the established rule; that they might behold and kiss for the last time the sole salvation of man, and obtain a provision for the passage to another life, in having the precious cross as their means of transport to the better lot. In performance of which request, Thomas brings forth the life-giving wood, announcing stated days for its display, that all the neighboring people might have an opportunity to assemble and enjoy the salvation thence proceeding.

Accordingly, my parents visited it together with the rest, accompanied by myself, at that time a school-boy. When, therefore, we requested permission to adore and kiss the precious cross, Thomas, lifting up both his hands, displayed the wood which blotted out the ancient curse, making an entire circuit of the sanctuary, as was customary on the ordinary days of adoration. As Thomas moved from place to place, there followed him a large body of fire, blazing but not consuming; so that the whole spot where he stood to display the precious cross seemed to be in flames: and this took place not once or twice but often, as the priest was making the circuit of the place, and the assembled people were entreating him that it might be done. This circumstance foreshowed the preservation which was granted to the Apameans. Accordingly, a representation of it was suspended on the roof of the sanctuary, explaining it by its delineation to those who were uninformed: which was preserved until the irruption of Adaarmanes and the Persians, when it was burnt together with the holy church in the conflagration of the entire city. Such were these events.

But Chosroes, in his retreat, acted in direct violation of conditions—for even on this occasion terms had been made—in a manner suited to his restless and inconstant disposition, but utterly unbecoming a rational man, much more a king professing a regard for treaties.

CHAPTER XXVII
SIEGE OF EDESSA BY CHOSROES.

The same Procopius narrates what the ancients had recorded concerning Edessa and Abgarus, and how Christ wrote a letter to him. He then relates how Chosroes made a fresh movement to lay siege to the city, thinking to falsify the assertion prevalent among the faithful, that Edessa would never fall into the power of an enemy: which assertion, however, is not contained in what was written to Abgarus by Christ our God; as the studious may gather from the history of Eusebius Pamphili, who cites the epistle verbatim. Such, however, is the averment and belief of the faithful; which was then realized, faith bringing about the accomplishment of the prediction. For after Chosroes had made many assaults on the city, had raised a mound of sufficient size to overtop the walls of the town, and had devised innumerable expedients beside, he raised the siege and retreated. I will, however, detail the particulars.

AD 540

Chosroes ordered his troops to collect a great quantity of wood for the siege from whatever timber fell in their way; and when this had been done before the order could well be issued, arranging it in a circular form, he threw a mound inside with its face advancing against the city. In this way elevating it gradually with the timber and earth, and pushing it forward towards the town, he raised it to a height sufficient to overtop the wall, so that the besiegers could hurl their missiles from vantage ground against the defenders. When the besiegers saw the mound approaching the walls like a moving mountain, and the enemy in expectation of stepping into the town at day-break, they devised to run a mine under the mound—which the Latins term "aggestus"—and by that means apply fire, so that the combustion of the timber might cause the downfall of the mound. The mine was completed;

but they failed in attempting to fire the wood, because the fire, having no exit whence it could obtain a supply of air, was unable to take hold of it.

In this state of utter perplexity, they bring the divinely wrought image, which the hands of men did not form, but Christ our God sent to Abgarus on his desiring to see Him.[5] Accordingly, having introduced this holy image into the mine, and washed it over with water, they sprinkled some upon the timber; and the divine power forthwith being present to the faith of those who had so done, the result was accomplished which had previously been impossible: for the timber immediately caught the flame, and being in an instant reduced to cinders, communicated with that above, and the fire spread in all directions. When the besieged saw the smoke rising, they adopted the following contrivance. Having filled small jars with sulphur, tow, and other combustibles, they threw them upon the aggestus; and these, sending forth smoke as the fire was increased by the force of their flight, prevented that which was rising from the mud from being observed; so that all who were not in the secret, supposed that the smoke proceeded solely from the jars. On the third day the flames were seen issuing from the earth, and then the Persians on the mound became aware of their unfortunate situation. But Chosroes, as if in opposition to the power of heaven, endeavored to extinguish the pile, by turning all the water-courses which were outside the city upon it. The fire, however, receiving the water as if it had been oil or sulphur, or some other combustible, continually increased, until it had completely levelled the entire mound and reduced the aggestus to ashes.

Then Chosroes, in utter despair, impressed by the circumstances with a sense of his disgraceful folly in having entertained an idea of prevailing over the God whom we worship, retreated ingloriously into his own territories.

CHAPTER XXVIII

MIRACLE AT SERGIOPOLIS.

What occurred at Sergiopolis through the proceedings of Chosroes shall also be described, as being a notable event and worthy of perpetual remembrance. Chosroes advanced against this city too, eager for its capture; and on his proceeding to assault the walls, negotiations took place with a view to spare the city: and it was agreed that the sacred treasures should be a ransom for the place, among which was also a cross presented by Justinian and Theodora. When they had been duly conveyed, Chosroes asked the priest and the Persians who had been sent with him, whether there was not any thing besides. Upon this one of them, being persons unaccustomed to speak the truth, told Chosroes that there were some other treasures concealed by the townsmen, who were but few. In fact, there had been left behind not any treasure of gold or silver, but one of more valuable material, and irrevocably devoted to God, namely, the holy relics of the victorious martyr Sergius, lying in a coffin of the oblong sort, plated over with silver.

Chosroes, influenced by these persons, advanced his whole army against the city; when suddenly there appeared along the circuit of the walls, in defense of the place, innumerable shields; on seeing which the persons sent by Chosroes returned, describing, with wonder, the number and fashion of the arms. And when, on further enquiry, he learned that very few persons remained in the city, and these consisted of aged people and children, from the absence of the flower of the population, he perceived that the prodigy proceeded from the martyr, and, influenced by fear and wonder at the faith of the Christians, he withdrew into his own country.

They also say that in his latter days he partook in the holy regeneration.

CHAPTER XXIX

PESTILENCE.

I will also describe the circumstances of the pestilence which commenced at that period, and has now prevailed and extended over the whole world for fifty-two years; a circumstance such as has never before been recorded.[6] Two years after the capture of Antioch by the Persians, a pestilence broke out, in some respects similar to that described by Thucydides, in others widely different. It took its rise from Ethiopia, as is now reported, and made a circuit of the whole world in succession, leaving, as I suppose, no part of the human race unvisited by the disease.

AD 542

Some cities were so severely afflicted as to be altogether depopulated, though in other places the visitation was less violent. It neither commenced according to any fixed period, nor was the time of its cessation uniform; but it seized upon some places at the commencement of winter, others in the course of the spring, others during the summer, and in some cases, when the autumn was advanced. In some instances, having infected a part of a city, it left the remainder untouched; and frequently in an uninfected city one might remark a few households excessively wasted; and in several places, while one or two households utterly perished, the rest of the city remained unvisited: but, as we have learned from careful observation, the uninfected households alone suffered the succeeding year. But the most singular circumstance of all was this; that if it happened that any inhabitants of an infected city were living in a place which the calamity had not visited, these alone were seized with the disorder. This visitation also befell cities and other places in many instances according to the periods called Indictions;[7] and the disease occurred, with the almost utter destruction of human beings, in the second year of each indiction.

Thus it happened in my own case—for I deem it fitting, in due adaptation of circumstances, to insert also in this history matters relating to myself—that at the commencement of this calamity, I was seized with what are termed buboes while still a school-boy, and lost by its recurrence at different times several of my children, my wife, and many of my kin, as well as of my domestic and country servants; the several indictions making, as it were, a distribution of my misfortunes. Thus, not quite two years before my writing this, being now in the fifty-eighth year of my age, on its fourth visit to Antioch, at the expiration of the fourth indiction from its commencement, I lost a daughter and her son, besides those who had died previously.

The plague was a complication of diseases: for, in some cases, commencing in the head, and rendering the eyes bloody and the face swollen, it descended into the throat, and then destroyed the patient. In others, there was a flux of the bowels: in others buboes were formed, followed by violent fever; and the sufferers died at the end of two or three days, equally in possession, with the healthy, of their mental and bodily powers. Others died in a state of delirium, and some by the breaking out of carbuncles. Cases occurred where persons who had been attacked once and twice and had recovered, died by a subsequent seizure.

The ways in which the disease was communicated were various and unaccountable: for some perished by merely living with the infected, others by only touching them, others by having entered their chamber, others by frequenting public places. Some, having fled from the infected cities, escaped themselves, but imparted the disease to the healthy. Some were altogether free from contagion, though they had associated with many who were afflicted, and had touched many not only in their sickness but also when dead. Some, too, who were desirous of death, on account of the utter loss of their children and friends, and with this view placed themselves as much as possible in contact with the diseased, were nevertheless not infected; as if the pestilence struggled against their purpose.

This calamity has prevailed, as I have already said, to the present time, for two and fifty years, exceeding all that have preceded it. For Philostratus expresses wonder that the pestilence which happened in his time, lasted for fifteen years. The sequel is uncertain, since its course will be guided by the good pleasure of God, who knows both the causes of things, and their tendencies. I shall now return to the point from which I digressed, and relate the remainder of Justinian's history.

CHAPTER XXX

AVARICE OF JUSTINIAN.

Justinian was insatiable in the acquisition of wealth, and so excessively covetous of the property of others, that he sold for money the whole body of his subjects to those who were entrusted with offices or who were collectors of tributes, and to whatever persons were disposed to entrap others by groundless charges. He stripped of their entire property innumerable wealthy persons, under color of the emptiest pretexts. If even a prostitute, marking out an individual as a victim, raised a charge of criminal intercourse against him, all law was at once rendered vain, and by making Justinian her associate in dishonest gain, she transferred to herself the whole wealth of the accused person.

At the same time he was liberal in expenditure; so far as to raise in every quarter many sacred and magnificent temples, and other religious edifices devoted to the care of infants and aged persons of either sex, and of such as were afflicted with various diseases. He also appropriated considerable revenues for carrying out these objects; and performed many such actions as are pious and acceptable to God, provided that those who perform them do so from their own means and the offering of their deeds be pure.

CHAPTER XXXI

DESCRIPTION OF THE CHURCH OF ST. SOPHIA AT CONSTANTINOPLE.

He also raised at Constantinople many sacred buildings of elaborate beauty, in honor of God and the saints, and erected a vast and incomparable work, such as has never been before recorded, namely the largest edifice of the Church, a noble and surpassing structure, beyond the power of words to describe. Nevertheless I will endeavor to the best of my ability to detail the plan of the sacred precinct.

The nave of the sanctuary is a dome, supported by four arches, and raised to so great a height, that the sight of persons surveying it from below can scarcely reach the vertex of the hemisphere, and no one from above, however daring, ventures to bend over and look down to the floor. The arches are raised clear from the pavement to the roof: but within those on the right and left are ranged columns of Thessalian stone, which, together with other corresponding pillars, support galleries, so as to allow those who wish, to look down upon the performance of the rites below. From these the empress also, when attending at the festivals, witnesses the ceremony of the sacred mysteries. But the eastern and western arches are left vacant, without, any thing to interrupt the imposing aspect of so vast dimensions. There are also colonnades under the before-mentioned galleries, forming, with pillars and small arches, a termination to so vast a structure.

But in order to convey a more distinct idea of this wonderful fabric, I have thought proper to set down in feet, its length, breadth, and height, as well as the span and height of the arches, as follows: The length from the door facing the sacred apse where are performed the rites of the bloodless sacrifice, to the apse is one hundred and ninety feet: the breadth from north to south is one hundred and fifteen feet:

the depth from the center of the hemisphere to the floor is one hundred and eighty feet: the span of each of the arches is * * * feet:[8] the length, however, from east to west is two hundred and sixty feet; and the range of the lights seventy-five feet. There are also to the west two other noble colonnades, and on all sides unroofed courts of elaborate beauty. Justinian also erected the church of the holy Apostles, which may dispute the first place with any other. In this the emperors and the bishops are usually interred. I have thought fit thus to take some notice of these and similar matters.

CHAPTER. XXXII

PARTIALITY OF JUSTINIAN FOR THE BLUE FACTION.

Justinian was possessed by another propensity of unequalled ferocity; whether attributable to an innate defect of his disposition, or to cowardice and apprehensions, I am not able to say. It took its rise from the existence of the faction among the populace distinguished by the name "Nika." He appeared to favor one party, namely the Blues, to such an excess, that they slaughtered their opponents at mid-day and in the middle of the city, and, so far from dreading punishment, were even rewarded; so that many persons became murderers from this cause. They were allowed to assault houses, to plunder the valuables they contained, and to compel persons to purchase their own lives; and if any of the authorities endeavored to check them, he was in danger of his very life: and it actually happened that a person holding the government of the East, having chastised some of the rioters with lashes, was himself scourged in the very center of the city, and carried about in triumph. Callinicus also, the governor of Cilicia, having subjected to legal punishment two Cilician murderers, Paul and Faustinus, who had assaulted and endeavored to dispatch him, suffered impalement, as the penalty for right feeling and maintenance of the laws.

The members of the other faction having, in consequence,

fled from their homes, and meeting with a welcome nowhere, but being universally scouted as a pollution, betook themselves to waylaying travellers, and committed thefts and murders to such an extent, that every place was filled with untimely deaths, robberies, and every other crime. Sometimes also, siding with the other faction, Justinian put to death in turn their opponents by surrendering to the vengeance of the laws those whom he had allowed to commit in the cities equal outrages with barbarians. Neither words nor time would suffice for a minute detail of these transactions. Thus much will, however, serve for a conception of the remainder.

CHAPTER XXXIII
BARSANUPHIUS THE ASCETIC.

There lived at that season men divinely inspired and workers of distinguished miracles in various parts of the world, but whose glory has shone forth everywhere. First, Barsanuphius, an Egyptian. He maintained in the flesh the exercise of the fleshless life, in a certain seat of contemplation near the town of Gaza, and succeeded in working wonders too numerous to be recorded. He is also believed to be still alive, enclosed in a chamber, although for fifty years and more from this time he has not been seen by any one, nor has he partaken of any earthly thing. When Eustochius, the president of the church of Jerusalem, in disbelief of this account, had determined to dig into the chamber where the man of God was enclosed, fire burst forth and nearly consumed all those who were on the spot.

CHAPTER XXXIV
SIMEON THE MONK.

There lived also at Emesa, Simeon, a man who had so completely unclothed himself of vain-glory as to appear insane to those who did not know him, although filled with all wisdom and divine grace. This Simeon lived principally in solitude, affording to none the means of knowing how and when he propitiated the Deity, nor his time of abstinence or eating. Frequently, too, on the public roads, he seemed to be deprived of self-possession, and to become utterly void of sense and intelligence, and entering at times into a tavern, he would eat, when he happened to be hungry, whatever food was within his reach. But if any one saluted him with an inclination of the head, he would leave the place angrily and hastily, through reluctance that his peculiar virtues should be detected by many persons. Such was the conduct of Simeon in public.

But there were some of his acquaintances, with whom he associated without any assumed appearances. One of his friends had a female domestic, who, having been debauched and become pregnant by some person, when she was urged by her owners to name the individual, said that Simeon had secretly cohabited with her and that she was pregnant by him; that she was ready to swear to the truth of this statement, and, if necessary, to convict him. On hearing this, Simeon assented, saying that he bore the flesh with its frailties; and when the story was universally spread, and Simeon, as it seemed, was deeply disgraced, he withdrew into retirement, as if from feelings of shame. When the woman's time had arrived, and she had been placed in the usual position, her throes, causing great and intolerable sufferings, brought her into imminent peril, but the birth made no progress. When, accordingly, they besought Simeon, who had come thither designedly to pray for her, he openly declared that the woman would not be delivered before she had said who was the father of the child: and when she had done this, and named the real father, the delivery was instantaneous, as though by the midwifery of truth.

He once was seen to enter the chamber of a courtesan, and having closed the door, he remained alone with her a considerable time; and when, again opening it, he went away looking round on all sides lest any one should see him, suspicion rose to so high a pitch, that those who witnessed it, brought out the woman, and inquired what was the nature of Simeon's visit to her and continuance with her for so long a time. She swore that, from want of necessaries, she had tasted nothing but water for three days past, and that Simeon had brought her victuals and a vessel of wine; that, having closed the door, he set a table before her and bid her make a meal, and satisfy her hunger, after her sufferings from want of food. She then produced the remains of what had been set before her.

Also at the approach of the earthquake which visited Phœnicia Maritima, and by which Berytus, Byblus, and Tripolis especially suffered, raising a whip in his hand, he struck the greater part of the columns in the forum, exclaiming, "Stand still, if there shall be occasion to dance." Inasmuch as none of his actions were unmeaning, those who were present carefully marked which were the columns he passed by without striking them. These were soon afterwards thrown down by the effects of the earthquake. Many other things he also did which require a separate treatise.

CHAPTER XXXV

THOMAS THE MONK.

At that time lived also Thomas, who pursued the same mode of life in Cœle-Syria. On occasion of his visiting Antioch, for the purpose of receiving the yearly stipend for the support of his monastery, which had been assigned from the revenues of the church in that place, Anastasius, the steward of the church, struck him on the head with his hand, because he frequently troubled him. When the bystanders manifested indignation, he said that neither himself should again receive nor Anastasius pay the money. Both which things came to pass, by the death of Anastasius after an interval of one day, and by the departure of Thomas to the unfading life, on his way back, in the sick hospital at the suburb of Daphne.

They deposited his body in the tomb appropriated to strangers: but, after the subsequent interment of two others, his body was found above them, an extraordinary wonder, proceeding from God, who bore testimony to him even after his death; for the other bodies were thrown to a considerable distance. They report the circumstance to Ephraemius, in admiration of the saint. In consequence, his holy body is transported to Antioch, with a public festival and procession, and is honored with a place in the cemetery, having, by its translation, stopped the plague which was then visiting the place. The yearly festival in honor of whom the sons of the Antiochenes continue to celebrate to our time with great magnificence. Let, me now, however, return to my subject.

CHAPTER XXXVI

ACCOUNT OF A MIRACLE IN THE PATRIARCHATE OF MENAS.

When Anthimus, as has been already mentioned, was removed from the see of the imperial city, Epiphanius succeeds to the bishopric; and after Epiphanius, Menas, in whose time also occurred a remarkable prodigy. It is an old custom in the imperial city, that when there remains over a considerable quantity of the holy fragments of the immaculate body of Christ our God, boys of tender age should be fetched from among those who attend the schools, to eat them. On one occasion of this kind, there was included among them the son of a glassworker, a Jew by faith; who, in reply to the inquiries of his parents respecting the cause of his delay, told them what had taken place, and what he had eaten in company with the other boys. The father, in his indignation and fury, places the boy in the furnace where he used to mould the glass. The mother, unable to find her child, wandered over the city with lamentations and wailings; and on the third day, standing by the door of her husband's workshop, was calling upon the boy by name, tearing herself in her sorrow. He, recognizing his mother's voice, answered her from within the furnace, and she, bursting open the doors, saw, on her entrance, the boy standing in the midst of the coals, and untouched by the fire. On being asked how he had continued unhurt, he said that a woman in a purple robe had frequently visited him; that she had offered him water, and with it had quenched that part of the coals which was nearest to him; and that she had supplied him with food as often as he was hungry.

Justinian, on the report of this occurrence, placed the boy and his mother in the orders of the church, after they had been enlightened by the laver of regeneration. But the father, on his refusal to be numbered among the Christians, he ordered to be impaled in the suburb of Sycæ, as being the murderer of his child.

Such was the course of these occurrences.

CHAPTER XXXVII
SUCCESSION OF BISHOPS.

After Menas, Eutychius is elevated to the see.

At Jerusalem, Sallustius succeeds Martyrius, who is himself succeeded by Helias. The next in succession was Peter; and after him came Macarius, without the emperor's confirmation. He was ejected from his see, on the charge of maintaining the opinions of Origen, and was succeeded by Eustochius. After the removal of Theodosius, as has been already mentioned, Zoilus is appointed bishop of Alexandria, and when he had been gathered to his predecessors, Apollinaris obtains the chair. After Ephraemius, Domninus is entrusted with the see of Antioch.

CHAPTER XXXVIII
THE FIFTH GENERAL COUNCIL.

During the time that Vigilius was bishop of the Elder Rome, and first Menas, then Eutychius of New Rome, Apollinaris of Alexandria, Domninus of Antioch, and Eustochius of Jerusalem, Justinian summons the fifth synod, for the following reason: On account of the increasing influence of those who held the opinions of Origen, especially in AD 552 what is called the New Laura, Eustochius used every effort for their removal, and, visiting the place itself, he ejected the whole party, driving them to a distance, as general pests. These persons, in their dispersion, associated with themselves many others. They found a champion in Theodore, surnamed Ascidas, bishop of Cæsarea, the metropolis of Cappadocia, who was constantly about the person of Justinian, as being trusty and highly serviceable to him. Whereas he was creating much confusion in the imperial court, and declared the proceeding of Eustochius to be utterly impious and lawless, the latter despatches to Constantinople Rufus, superior of the monastery of Theodosius, and Conon, of that of Saba, persons of the first distinction among the solitaries, both on account of their personal worth and the religious houses of which they were the heads; and with them were associated others scarcely their inferiors in dignity. These, in the first instance, mooted the questions relating to Origen, Evagrius, and Didymus. But Theodore of Cappadocia, with a view to divert them from this point, introduces the subject of Theodore of Mopsuestia, Theodoret, and Ibas; the good God providentially disposing the whole proceeding, in order that the profanities of both parties should be ejected.

On the first question being started, namely, whether it were proper to anathematize the dead, Eutychius, a man of consummate skill in the divine Scriptures, being as yet an undistinguished person—for Menas was still living, and he was himself at that time apocrisiarius to the bishop of Amasea—casting a look on the assembly, not merely of commanding intelligence but of contempt, plainly declared that the question needed no debate, since King Josiah in former time not only slew the living priests of the demons, but also broke up the sepulchers of those who had long been dead. This was considered by all to have been spoken to the purpose. Justinian also, having been made acquainted with the circumstance, elevated him to the see of the imperial city on the death of Menas, which happened immediately after. Vigilius gave his assent, in writing to the assembling of the synod but declined attendance.

Justinian addressed an inquiry to the synod on its assembling, as to what was their opinion concerning Theodore, and the expressions of Theodoret against Cyril and his twelve chapters, as well as the epistle of Ibas, as it is termed, addressed to Maris, the Persian. After the reading of many passages of Theodore and Theodoret, and proof given that Theodore had been long ago condemned and erased from the sacred diptychs, as also that it was fitting that heretics should be condemned after their death, they unanimously anathematize Theodore, and what had been advanced by Theodoret against the twelve chapters of Cyril and the right, faith; as also the epistle of Ibas to Maris, the Persian; in the following words:

"Our great God and Savior Jesus Christ, according to the parable in the gospels," and so forth. "In addition to all other heretics, who have been condemned and anathematized by the before-mentioned four holy synods and by the holy catholic and apostolic church, we condemn and anathematize Theodore, styled bishop of Mopsuestia, and his impious writings; also whatever has been impiously written by Theodoret against the right faith, against the twelve chapters of the sainted Cyril, and against the first holy synod at Ephesus, and all that he has written in defense of Theodore and Nestorius. We further anathematize the impious epistle said to have been written by Ibas to Maris the Persian."

After some other matter, they proceed to set forth fourteen chapters concerning the right and unimpeachable faith. In this manner had the transactions proceeded: but on the presentation of libels against the doctrine of Origen, named also Adamantius, and the followers of his impious error, by the monks Eulogius, Conon, Cyriacus, and Pancratius, Justinian addresses a question to the synod concerning these points, appending to it a copy of the libel, as well as the epistle of Vigilius upon the subject: from the whole of which may be gathered the attempts of Origen to fill the simplicity of the apostolic doctrine with philosophic and Manichæan tares. Accordingly, a relation was addressed to Justinian by the synod, after they had uttered exclamations against Origen and the maintainers of similar errors. A portion of it is expressed in the following terms:

"O most Christian emperor, gifted with heavenly generosity of soul," and so forth. "We have shunned, accordingly, we have shunned this error; for we knew not the voice of the alien; and having bound such a one, as a thief and a robber, in the cords of our anathema, we have ejected him from the sacred precincts." And presently they proceed: "By perusal you will learn the vigor of our acts." To this they appended a statement of the heads of the matters which the followers of Origen were taught to maintain, showing their agreements, as well as their disagreements, and their manifold errors.

The fifth head contains the blasphemous expressions uttered by private individuals belonging to what is called the New Laura, as follows. Theodore, surnamed Ascidas, the Cappadocian, said "If the Apostles and Martyrs at the present time work miracles, and are already so highly honored, unless they shall be equal with Christ in the restitution of things, in what respect is there a restitution for them?" They also reported many other blasphemies of Didymus, Evagrius, and Theodore; having with great diligence extracted whatever bore upon these points. At an interval of some time after the meeting of the synod, Eutychius is ejected, and there is appointed in his place to the see of Constantinople John a native of Seremis, which is a village of the district of Cynegica, belonging to Antioch.

CHAPTER XXXIX

DEPARTURE OF JUSTINIAN FROM ORTHODOXY.

At that time Justinian, abandoning the right road of doctrine, and following a path untrodden by the apostles and fathers, became entangled among thorns and briers; and wishing to fill the Church with them also, he failed in his purpose, and thereby fulfilled the prediction of prophecy; the Lord having secured the royal road with an unfailing fence, that murderers might not leap, as it were, upon a tottering wall or a broken hedge.

Thus, at the time when John, named also Catelinus, was bishop of the elder Rome, after Vigilius; John from Seremis of New Rome; Apollinaris, of Alexandria; Anastasius, of Theopolis, after Domninus; and Macarius, of Jerusalem, had been restored to his see; Justinian, after he had anathematized Origen, Didymus, and Evagrius, issued what the Latins call an Edict, after the deposition of Eustochius in which he termed the body of the Lord incorruptible and incapable of the natural and blameless passions affirming that the Lord ate before his passion in the same manner as after his resurrection, his holy body having undergone no conversion or change from the time of its actual formation in the womb, not even in respect, of the voluntary and natural passions, nor yet, after the resurrection. To this, he proceeded to compel the bishops in all quarters to give their assent. However, they all professed to look to Anastasius, the bishop of Antioch, and thus avoided the first attack.

CHAPTER XL

ANASTASIUS, PATRIARCH OF ANTIOCH.

Anastasius was a man most accomplished in divine learning, and so strict in his manners and mode of life as to insist upon very minute matters, and on no occasion to deviate from a staid and settled frame, much less in things of moment and having relation to the Deity himself. So well tempered was his character, that neither, by being accessible and affable, was he exposed to the intrusion of things unsuitable; nor by being austere and unindulgent, did he become difficult of approach for proper purposes. Accordingly, in serious concerns he was ready in ear and fluent in tongue, promptly resolving the questions proposed to him; but in trifling matters, his ears were altogether closed, and a bridle restrained his tongue, so that speech was enthralled by thought, and silence resulted, more valuable than speech.

Justinian assaults him, like some impregnable tower, with every kind of device, considering that if he could only succeed in shaking this bulwark, all difficulty would be removed in capturing the city, enslaving the right doctrine, and taking captive the sheep of Christ. In such a manner was AD 561 Anastasius raised above the assailing force by heavenly greatness of mind, for he stood upon the immovable rock of faith, that he unreservedly contradicted Justinian by a formal declaration, in which he showed very clearly and forcibly that the body of the Lord was corruptible in respect of the natural and blameless passions, and that the divine apostles and the inspired fathers both held and delivered this opinion. In the same terms he replied to a question of the monastic body of Syria Prima and Secunda, confirming the minds of all, preparing them for the struggle, and daily reading in the Church those words of the "chosen vessel:"[8] "If any one is preaching to you a gospel different from that which ye have received, even though it be an angel from heaven, let him be accursed."[10] To this all, with few exceptions, paid a steady regard and zealous adherence. He also addressed to the Antiochenes a valedictory discourse, on hearing that Justinian intended to banish him; a discourse deserving admiration for its elegance, its flow of thought, the abundance of sacred texts, and the appropriateness of its historical matters.

CHAPTER XLI

DEATH OF JUSTINIAN.

But this discourse was not published, "God having provided some better thing for us:"[11] for Justinian, while dictating the banishment of Anastasius and his associate priests, AD 565 departed this life by an invisible stroke, having reigned in all eight and thirty years and eight months.

NOTES

1.   Walford's original text had "Justin" here instead of "Justinian" but this is quite obviously an error.
2.   The word "nika" (νικα) in Greek is translated "victory" or "conquer." Evagrius drew his summary of the riots from the extensive account found in the *History of the Wars* of Procopius (Book I, xxiv, pp. 219– 239). Another account may be found in the Chronicle of John Malalas (Book 18, pp. 275–281).
3.   Evagrius refers here to the notorious John the Cappadocian who was Prætorian Prefect from AD 531 through 541.
4.   Evagrius makes an error here. Amalasuntha was, in reality, the daughter of Theodoric and Athalaric his grandson. See Procopius, *History of the Wars*, Book V, ii, pp. 15.
5.   This passage is the earliest known reference to the relic known as the Mandylion of Edessa, an image of Christ which is identified by some scholars with the Shroud of Turin (see Ian Wilson's *The Blood and the Shroud*). Other scholars, conversely, have attempted to demonstrate that this episode involving the image in Evagrius was the addition of later copyists. For a discussion, see Whitby, appendix II, pp. 323–326.
6.   The pestilence described by Evagrius here is widely regarded as the first outbreak of bubonic plague. Procopius describes it as a plague so horrible "that the whole human race came near to being annihilated" (Book II, xxii, p. 451).
7.   The Indiction was a taxation cycle lasting fifteen years. Obsolete by the time of Evagrius, it was nonetheless still used as a method of chronological reckoning (Bury, vol. 1, p. 47).
8.   There is a lacuna in the text here. At any rate, the dimensions of Hagia Sophia described here by Evagrius are largely inaccurate. For a discussion, see Whitby, p. 235, fn 95.
9.   Acts iv. 15.
10.   Gal. i. 9.
11.   Heb. xi. 40.

THE FIFTH BOOK

CHAPTER I

ACCESSION OF JUSTIN THE SECOND.

In this manner did Justinian depart to the lowest region of retribution, after having filled every place with confusion and tumults, and having received at the close of his life the reward of his actions. His nephew Justin succeeds to the purple; having previously held the office of guardian of the palace, styled in the Latin language Curopalata. No one, except those who were immediately about his person, was aware of the demise of Justinian or the declaration of Justin, until the latter made his appearance in the hippodrome, by way of formally assuming the stated functions of royalty. Confining himself to this simple proceeding, he then returned to the palace.

His first edict was one dismissing the bishops to their respective sees, wherever they might be assembled, with a provision that they should maintain what was already established in religion, and abstain from novelties in matters of faith. This proceeding was to his honor. In his mode of life, however, he was dissolute, utterly abandoned to luxury and inordinate pleasures: and to such a degree was he inflamed with desire for the property of others, as to convert every thing into a means of unlawful gain; standing in no awe of the Deity even in the case of bishoprics, but making them a matter of public sale to any purchasers that offered. Possessed, as he was, alike by the vices of audacity and cowardice, he in the first place sends for his kinsman Justin, a man universally famous for military skill and his other distinctions, who was at that time stationed upon the Danube, and engaged in preventing the Avars from crossing that river.

These were one of those Scythian tribes who live in wagons, and inhabit the plains beyond the Caucasus. Having been worsted by their neighbors, the Turks, they had migrated in a mass to the Bosphorus; and, having subsequently left the shores of the Euxine—where were many barbarian tribes, and where also cities, castles, and some harbors had been located by the Romans, being either settlements of veterans, or colonies sent out by the emperors—they were pursuing their march, in continual conflict with the barbarians whom they encountered, until they reached the bank of the Danube; and thence they sent an embassy to Justinian.

From this quarter Justin was summoned, as having a claim to the fulfillment of the terms of the agreement between himself and the emperor. For, since both of them had been possessed of equal dignity, and the succession to the empire was in suspense between both, they had agreed, after much dispute, that whichever of the two should become possessed of the sovereignty, should confer the second place on the other; so that while ranking beneath the emperor, he should still take precedence of all others.

CHAPTER II

MURDER OF JUSTINIAN, KINSMAN OF THE EMPEROR.

The emperor accordingly received him, in the first instance, with an abundant display of kindness. Afterwards, he proceeded to fix certain charges upon him, and to withdraw the various guards of his person, forbidding him at the same time access to his presence; for he himself lived in the retirement of his palace: and ultimately he ordered his removal to Alexandria. There he is miserably murdered in the dead of night, when he had just retired to rest; such being the reward of his fidelity to the commonwealth and his achievements in war. Nor did the emperor and his consort Sophia abate their rage, nor had they sufficiently indulged their boiling spite, before they had gazed upon his head and spurned it with their feet.

CHAPTER III

EXECUTION OF ÆTHERIUS AND ADDÆUS.

Not long after, the emperor brought to trial for treason Ætherius and Addæus, members of the senate, who had occupied the very highest position at the court of Justinian. Ætherius confessed to a design of poisoning the emperor, saying that he had in Addæus an accomplice in the plot and an abettor throughout. The latter, however, asseverated with fearful imprecations that he was utterly ignorant of the transaction. Both were accordingly beheaded, Addæus affirming, at the instant of execution, that he had been falsely accused on this point, but admitting that he received his due at the hands of all-seeing Justice, for that he had taken off Theodotus, prefect of the palace, by sorcery. How far these statements are true, I am not able to say; but both were men of bad character; Addæus being addicted to unnatural lust, and Ætherius pursuing to the utmost a system of false accusation, and plundering the property both of the living and the dead, in the name of the imperial household, of which he had been comptroller in the time of Justinian. Such was the termination of these matters.

CHAPTER IV

EDICT OF JUSTIN CONCERNING THE FAITH.

Justin issues an edict to the Christians in every quarter, in the following terms.

"In the name of the Lord Jesus Christ, our God, the Emperor Cæsar Flavian Justin, faithful in Christ, clement, supreme, beneficent, Alemannicus, Gothicus, Germanicus, Anticus, Francicus, Herulicus, Gepidicus, pious, fortunate, glorious, victorious, triumphant, ever-worshipful Augustus.

"'My peace I give to you,' says the Lord Christ, our very God. 'My peace I leave to you,' he also proclaims to all mankind. Now this is nothing else than that those who believe in him should gather into one and the same church, being unanimous concerning the true belief of Christians, and withdrawing from such as affirm or entertain contrary opinions: for the prime means of salvation for all men is the confession of the right faith. Wherefore we also, following the evangelical precepts and the holy symbol or doctrine of the holy fathers, exhort all persons to unite in one and the same church and sentiment; and this we do, believing in the Father, Son, and Holy Spirit, holding the doctrine of a consubstantial Trinity, one Godhead or nature and substance, both in terms and reality; one power, influence, and operation in three subsistences or persons; into which doctrine we were baptized, in which we believe, and to which we have united ourselves.

AD 566

For we worship a Unity in trinity and a Trinity in unity, peculiar both in its division and in its union, being Unity in respect of substance or Godhead, and Trinity with regard to its proprieties or subsistences or persons; for it is divided indivisibly, so to speak, and is united divisively: for there is one thing in three, namely, the Godhead; and the three things are one, namely, those in which is the Godhead, or, to speak more accurately, which are the Godhead: and we acknowledge the Father to be God, the Son God, and the Holy Spirit God, whenever each person is regarded by itself—the thought in that case separating the things that are inseparable—and the three when viewed in conjunction to be God by sameness of motion and of nature; inasmuch as it is proper both to confess the one God, and at the same time to proclaim the three subsistences or proprieties.

We also confess the only begotten Son of God, the God-Word, who, before the ages and without time, was begotten of the Father, not made, and who, in the last of the days, for our sakes and for our salvation, descended from heaven, and was incarnate of the Holy Spirit and of our Lady, the holy glorious Mother of God and ever virgin Mary, and was born of her; who is our Lord Jesus Christ, one of the Holy Trinity, united in glorification with the Father and the Holy Spirit: for the Holy Trinity did not admit the addition of a fourth person, even when one of the Trinity, the God-Word, had become incarnate; but our Lord Jesus Christ is one and the same, being consubstantial with God the Father, as respects the Godhead, and at the same time consubstantial with ourselves as respects the manhood; passible in the flesh, and at the same time impassible in the Godhead: for we do not admit that the divine Word who wrought the miracles was one, and he who underwent the sufferings was another; but we confess our Lord Jesus Christ to be one and the same, namely, the Word of God become incarnate and made perfectly man, and that both the miracles and the sufferings which he voluntarily underwent for our salvation belong to one and the same; inasmuch as it was not a human being that gave himself on our behalf; but, the God-Word himself, becoming man without undergoing change, submitted in the flesh to the voluntary passion and death on our behalf.

Accordingly, while confessing him to be God, we do not contravene the circumstance of his being man and while confessing him to be man, we do not deny the fact of his being

God: whence, while confessing our Lord Jesus Christ to be one and the same, composed of both natures, namely, the Godhead and the manhood, we do not superinduce confusion upon the union; for he will not lose the circumstance of being God on becoming man like ourselves; nor yet, in being by nature God, and in that respect, incapable of likeness to us, will he also decline the circumstance of being man. But as he continued God in manhood; in like manner, though possessed of divine supremacy, he is no less man; being both in one, God and man at the same time, one Emmanuel. Further, while confessing him to be at the same time perfect in Godhead and perfect in manhood, of which two he was also composed, we do not attach to his one complex subsistence a division by parts or severance; but we signify that the difference of the natures is not annulled by the union: for neither was the divine nature changed into the human, nor the human nature converted into the divine; but, each being the more distinctly understood and existent in the limit and relation of its own nature, we say that the union took place according to subsistence.

The union according to subsistence signifies, that the God-Word, that is to say one subsistence of the three subsistences of the Godhead, was not united with a previously existing human being, but in the womb of our Lady, the holy glorious Mother of God and ever virgin Mary, formed for himself of her, in his own subsistence, fresh consubstantial with ourselves, having the same passions in all respects except sin, and animated with a reasonable and intelligent soul; for he retained his subsistence in himself, and became man, and is one and the same, our Lord Jesus Christ, united in glorification with the Father and the Holy Spirit. Further, while considering his ineffable union, we rightly confess one nature, that of the Divine Word, to have become incarnate, by flesh animated with a reasonable and intelligent soul; and, on the other hand, while contemplating the difference of the natures, we affirm that they are two, without, however, introducing any division, for either nature is in him; whence we confess one and the same Christ, one Son, one person, one subsistence, both God and man together: and all who have held or do hold opinions at variance with these, we anathematize, judging them to be alien from the Holy and Apostolic Church of God.

Accordingly, while the right doctrines which have been delivered to us by the holy fathers are being thus proclaimed, we exhort you all to gather into one and the same Catholic and Apostolic Church, or rather we even entreat you; for though possessed of imperial supremacy, we do not decline the use of such a term, in behalf of the unanimity and union of all Christians, in the universal offering of one doxology to our great God and Savior Jesus Christ, and in abstinence for the future on the part of all from unnecessary disputes about persons and words—since the words lead to one true belief, and understanding—while the usage and form which has hitherto prevailed in the holy Catholic and Apostolic Church of God, remains for ever unshaken and unchanged."

To this edict all assented, saying that it was expressed in orthodox language. None, however, of the severed portions of the Church were entirely reunited, because the edict distinctly declared that what had hitherto been unshaken and unchanged, should continue so in all coming time.

CHAPTER V

DEPOSITION OF ANASTASIUS, PATRIARCH OF ANTIOCH.

Justin also ejected Anastasius from the episcopate of Theopolis, on the charge of profuse and improper expenditure of the funds of the see, and also for scandalous language against himself; inasmuch as Anastasius, on being asked why he was so lavishly squandering the property of the see, frankly replied, that it was done to prevent its being carried off by that universal pest, Justin. He is also said to have entertained a grudge against Anastasius, because he had refused to pay a sum of money, when demanded of him in consideration of his appointment to the bishopric. Other charges were also brought against him by persons, who, as I suppose, wished to second the emperor's bent.

CHARTER VI

GREGORY, THE SUCCESSOR OF ANASTASIUS.

Next in succession, Gregory is elevated to the episcopal see: "wide whose renown," according to the language of poetry; a person who had devoted himself from the earliest period of life to the monastic discipline, and had wrestled therein so manfully and stoutly, that he arrived at the highest

AD 572

elevation when scarcely past his boyhood, and became superior of the monastery of the Byzantines, in which he had assumed the bare mode of life, and subsequently, by the orders of Justin, of the monastery of Mount Sinai. Here he encountered extreme danger, having sustained a siege by the Scenite Arabs.

Having, nevertheless, secured the complete tranquillity of the spot, he was thence summoned to the archiepiscopal dignity. He was unrivalled in every excellence of intellect and virtue, and most energetic in accomplishing whatever he resolved upon, uninfluenced by fear, and incapable of shrinking before secular power. So noble was his expenditure of money, in a general system of liberality and munificence, that whenever he appeared in public, crowds, besides his ordinary attendants, followed him; and all gathered round him who saw or heard of his approach. The respect shown to so high a dignity, was but second to the honor bestowed upon the individual, in the generous desire of persons to obtain a near view of him and to hear his words; for he was possessed of singular power to inspire with attachment towards himself all who held converse with him, being a person of most imposing aspect and sweet address, especially quick of perception and prompt in execution, a most able counsellor and judge, both in his own matters and in those of others. On this account it was that he accomplished so much, never deferring any thing till tomorrow. By dealing with matters with unfailing promptitude, according as either necessity required or opportunity favored, he filled with admiration not only the Roman but the Persian sovereigns, as I shall set forth the particulars in their proper place. His character was strongly marked by vehemence, and at times by indications of anger; while, on the other hand, his meekness and gentleness were not confined, but were exceedingly abundant; so that to him was admirably fitted the excellent expression of Gregory Theologus, "austerity tempered with modesty," while neither quality was impaired, but each rendered more striking by the other.

CHAPTER VII

SUBMISSION OF THE INHABITANTS OF PERSARMENIA.

In the first year of the episcopate of Gregory, the inhabitants of what was formerly called the greater Armenia, but afterwards Persarmenia—this country was formerly subject to the Romans, but when Philip, the successor of Gordian, had betrayed it to Sapor, what is called the lesser Armenia alone was possessed by the Romans, but the remainder by the Persians—this people, being Christians and cruelly treated by the Persians, especially on the score of their faith, sent a secret embassy to Justin, imploring to be allowed to place themselves under the dominion of the Romans, in order to [enjoy][1] a safe and unrestrained observance of their religion.

When the emperor had admitted their overtures, and certain written conditions had been settled on his part and guaranteed by the most solemn oaths, the Armenians massacre their governors; and the whole nation, together with their allied neighbors, both of kindred and foreign AD 572 race, unite themselves to the Roman empire, Vardanes having a precedence among his countrymen by birth, dignity, and military skill. In reply to the complaints of Chosroes on account of these transactions, Justin alleged that the peace had expired, and that it was impossible to reject the advances of Christians, when desirous of uniting themselves with fellow Christians in time of war.

Such was his reply. Notwithstanding, he made no preparation for war, but was involved in his habitual luxury, regarding every thing as secondary to his personal enjoyments.

CHAPTER VIII

SIEGE OF NISIBIS BY MARCIAN.

The emperor sends out his kinsman Marcian as commander of the forces of the East without, however, sufficiently supplying him with troops, or the other material of war. He occupies Mesopotamia, at the imminent risk of utter ruin, followed by very few troops, and these imperfectly armed, and by a few rustic laborers and herdsmen, whom he had pressed into his service from among the provincials. After gaining the advantage in some skirmishes near Nisibis with the Persians, who were themselves not yet completely prepared, he sits down before that city, though the enemy did not think it necessary to close the gates, and insolently jeered the Roman troops. Besides many other prodigies presaging the approaching calamities, I also saw, at the beginning of the war, a newly born calf with two heads.

CHAPTER IX

INVASION OF THE PERSIANS.

Chosroes, when his preparations for war were completed, having accompanied Adaarmanes for some distance, AD 574 sent him across the Euphrates from his own bank of the river into the Roman territory, by Circesium, a city most important to the Romans, situated at the limit of the empire, and rendered strong not only by its walls, which are carried to an immense height, but by the rivers Euphrates and Aboras, which, as it were, insulate the place. Chosroes himself, having crossed the Tigris with his own division of the army, advanced upon Nisibis.

Of these operations the Romans were for a long time ignorant, so far that Justin, relying on a rumor to the effect that Chosroes was either dead or approaching his last breath, was indignant at the tardiness of the siege of Nisibis, and sent persons for the purpose of stimulating the efforts of Marcian, and bringing to him the keys of the gates as quickly as possible. Information, however, that the siege was making no progress, but that the commander was bringing great discredit upon himself by attempting impossibilities in the case of so important a city with so contemptible a force, is conveyed in the first instance to Gregory, bishop of Theopolis: for the bishop of Nisibis, being strongly attached to Gregory, as having received munificent presents from him, and especially being indignant at the insolence which the Persians were continually displaying towards the Christians, and desirous that his city should be subject to the Roman power, supplied information to Gregory of all things that were going on in the enemy's territory, at each several juncture. This the latter immediately forwarded to Justin, informing him as quickly as possible of the advance of Chosroes: but he, being immersed in his habitual pleasures, paid no regard to the letters of Gregory; nor was he indeed inclined to believe them, indulging rather the thoughts suggested by his wishes: for the ordinary mark of dissolute persons is a meanness of spirit combined with confidence with regard to results; as well as incredulity, if any thing occurs which runs counter to their desires. Accordingly he writes to Gregory, altogether repudiating the information as being utterly false, and, even supposing it were true, saying that the Persians would not come up before the siege was concluded, and that, if they did, they would be beaten off with loss. He further sends Acacius, a wicked and insolent man, to Marcian with orders to supersede him in the command, even supposing he had already set one foot within the town. This command he strictly executed, carrying out the emperor's order without any regard to the public good: for, on his arrival at the camp, he deprives Marcian of his command while on the enemy's territory, and without informing the army of the transaction. The various officers, on learning at the break of the next day that their commander was superseded, no longer appeared at the head of their troops, but stole away in various directions and thus raised that ridiculous siege.

Adaarmanes, on the other hand, in command of a considerable force of Persians and Scenite barbarians, having marched by Circesium, inflicted every possible injury with fire and sword upon the Roman territory, setting no limits to his intentions or actions. He also captures many fortresses and towns, without encountering any resistance; in the first place, because there was no one in command, and secondly, because, since the Roman troops were shut up in Daras by Chosroes, his foragings and incursions were made in perfect security.

He also directed an advance upon Theopolis, without proceeding thither in person. These troops were compelled to draw off most unexpectedly; for scarcely any one, or indeed very few persons, remained in the city; and the bishop had fled, taking with him the sacred treasures, because both the greater part of the walls had fallen to ruins, and the populace had made insurrection with the hope of gaining ascendancy by change: a thing of frequent occurrence, and especially at junctures like this. The insurgents themselves also abandoned the city, without any attempt to meet the emergency or take active measures against the enemy.

CHAPTER X

CAPTURE OF APAMEA AND DARAS.

Failing thus in this attempt, Adaarmanes, having burnt the city formerly called Heraclea but subsequently Gagalica, made himself master of Apamea; which, having been founded by Seleucus Nicator, was once flourishing and populous, but had fallen to a great extent into ruin through lapse of time. On the capitulation of the city from the inability of the inhabitants to offer any resistance, since the wall had fallen down through age, he fired and pillaged the whole place, in violation of the terms, and drew off, carrying away captive the inhabitants of the town and the adjoining country, and among them the bishop and the governor. He also exercised every kind of atrocity during his march, without meeting with any resistance or indeed attempt at opposition, except a very small force sent out by Justin under the command of Magnus, who had formerly been a banker at Constantinople, and subsequently appointed steward of one of the imperial residences. These troops however fled with precipitation, and narrowly escaped being made prisoners.

After these operations, Adaarmanes joins Chosroes, who had not yet captured the city he was besieging. By the junction, he threw an important weight into the scale, in raising the spirits of his countrymen, while he disheartened their opponents. He found the city cut off by lines, and a huge mound carried forward within a short distance of the walls, with engines mounted, and especially catapults, shooting from vantage ground. By these means, Chosroes took the city by storm. John, the son of Timostratus, was governor, who paid little regard to the defense of the place, or perhaps betrayed it; for both accounts are reported. Chosroes had besieged the city for five months or more without any effort being made for its relief. Having brought forth all the inhabitants in immense numbers, some of whom he miserably slaughtered but retained the greater part as captives, he garrisoned the city, on account of its important situation, and then retired into his own territories.

CHAPTER XI

INSANITY OF JUSTIN.

On being informed of these events, Justin, in whose mind no sober and considerate thoughts found place after so much inflation and pride, and who did not bear what had befallen him with resignation suited to a human being, falls into a state of frenzy, and becomes unconscious of all subsequent transactions.

Tiberius assumes the direction of affairs, a Thracian by birth, but holding the first place in the court of Justin. He had previously been sent out against the Avars by the emperor, who had raised a very large army for the purpose; and he would inevitably have been made prisoner, since his troops would not even face the barbarians, had not divine Providence unexpectedly delivered him, and preserved him for succession to the Roman sovereignty; which, through the inconsiderate measures of Justin, was in danger of falling to ruin, together with the entire commonwealth, and of passing from such a height of power into the hands of barbarians.

CHAPTER XII

EMBASSY OF TRAJAN TO CHOSROES.

Accordingly, Tiberius adopts a measure opportune and well suited to the state of affairs, which altogether repaired the calamity. He despatches to Chosroes, Trajan, a senator and an accomplished man, universally esteemed for his years and intelligence; not, however, as representative of the sovereign power, nor yet as ambassador for the commonwealth, but merely to treat on behalf of the empress Sophia; who herself also wrote to Chosroes, bewailing the calamities which had befallen her husband, and the loss of its head which the commonwealth sustained, and urging the unseemliness of trampling upon a widowed female, a prostrate monarch, and a desolate empire: at the same time reminding him that, when afflicted with sickness, he had himself not only been treated with similar forbearance, but that the very best physicians had been sent to him by the Roman government, and had cured him of his disease. Chosroes is, accordingly, moved by the appeal, and when upon the very point of attacking the empire, makes a truce for three years, embracing the eastern parts; with a condition that Armenia should be excepted, so as to allow of hostilities being maintained there, provided the East were not molested.

During these proceedings in the East, Sirmium is taken by the barbarians, which had some time before fallen into the hands of the Gepidæ and been afterwards restored by them to Justin.

CHAPTER XIII

PROCLAMATION OF TIBERIUS. HIS CHARACTER.

About this time Justin, by the advice of Sophia, bestows on Tiberius the rank of Cæsar, giving utterance, in the act of declaration, to such expressions as surpass all that has been recorded in ancient or recent history; our compassionate God having vouchsafed to him an opportunity for an avowal of his own errors, and a suggestion of AD 574 what was for the benefit of the state. For when there were assembled in the open court, where ancient usage enjoins that such proceedings should take place, both the archbishop, John, whom we have already mentioned, and his clergy, as well as the state dignitaries, and the household troops the emperor, on investing Tiberius with the imperial tunic and robe, gave utterance with a loud voice to the following words:

"Let not the grandeur of thy investiture deceive thee, nor the pomp of the present spectacle; beguiled by which,

I have unwittingly rendered myself obnoxious to the most severe penalties. Do thou make reparation for my errors, by administering the commonwealth with all gentleness." Then pointing to the magistrates, he recommended him by no means to put confidence in them, adding: "These are the very persons who have brought me into the condition which thou now witnessest:" together with other similar expressions, which filled all with utter amazement, and drew forth an abundance of tears.

Tiberius was very tall, and by far the most noble in person not only of sovereigns but all mankind; so that, in the first place, his beauty was deserving of sovereignty. In disposition, he was mild and compassionate, and gave cordial reception to all persons at their very first approach. He deemed wealth to consist in aiding all with largesses, not merely so far as to meet their wants, but even to superfluity: for he did not consider what the needy ought to receive, but what it became a Roman emperor to bestow. He esteemed that gold to be adulterated which was exacted with tears: on which account he entirely remitted the taxation for one year, and released from their imposts the properties which Adaarmanes had devastated, not merely to the extent of the damage but even far beyond it. The magistrates were also excused from the necessity of making the unlawful presents, by means of which the emperors formerly made a sale of their subjects. On these points he also issued constitutions, as a security for coming time.

CHAPTER XIV

SUCCESSES OF THE ROMAN COMMANDER JUSTINIAN AGAINST THE PERSIANS.

Tiberius, accordingly, applying to a rightful purpose the wealth which had been amassed by improper means, made the necessary preparations for war. So numerous was the army of brave men, raised among the Transalpine nations, the Massagetæ, and other

Scythian tribes, by a choice levy in the countries on the Rhine, and on this side of the Alps, as well as in Pæonia, Mysia, Illyria, and Isauria, that he completed squadrons of excellent cavalry, to the amount of nearly one hundred and fifty thousand men, and repulsed Chosroes, who, immediately after the capture of Daras, had advanced in the course of the summer against Armenia, and was thence directing his movements upon Cæsarea, which was the seat of government of Cappadocia and the capital of the cities in that quarter.

In such contempt did Chosroes hold the Roman power, that, when the Cæsar had sent an embassy to him, he did not deign to admit the ambassadors to an audience, but bid them follow him to Cæsarea; at which place he said he would take the embassy into his consideration. When, AD 576 however, he saw the Roman army in the front of him, under the command of Justinian, the brother of that Justin who had been miserably put to death by the Emperor Justin, in complete equipment, with the trumpets sending forth martial sounds, the standards uplifted for conflict, and the soldiery eager for slaughter, breathing forth fury, and at the same time maintaining perfect order, and, besides, so numerous and noble a body of cavalry as no monarch had ever imagined, he drew a deep groan, with many adjurations, at the unforeseen and unexpected sight, and was reluctant to begin the engagement. But while he is lingering and whiling away the time, and making a mere feint of fighting, Kurs, the Scythian, who was in command of the right wing, advances upon him; and since the Persians were unable to stand his charge, and were in a very signal manner abandoning their ground, he made an extensive slaughter of his opponents. He also attacks the rear, where both Chosroes and the whole army had placed their baggage, and captures all the royal stores and the entire baggage, under the very eyes of Chosroes; who endured the sight, deeming self-imposed constraint more tolerable than the onset of Kurs. The latter, having together with his troops made himself master of a great amount of money and spoil, and carrying off the beasts of burden with their loads, among which was the sacred fire of Chosroes to which divine honors were paid, makes a circuit of the Persian camp, singing songs of victory, and rejoins, about nightfall, his own army, who had already broken up from their position, without a commencement of battle on the part of either Chosroes or themselves, beyond a few slight skirmishes or single combats, such as usually take place.

Chosroes, having lighted many fires, made preparations for a night assault; and since the Romans had formed two camps, he attacks the division which lay northward, at the dead of night. On their giving way under this sudden and unexpected onset, he advances upon the neighboring town of Melitene, which was undefended and deserted by its inhabitants, and having fired the whole place, prepared to cross the Euphrates. At the approach, however, of the united forces of the Romans, in alarm for his own safety, he mounted an elephant, and crossed alone; while great numbers of his army found a grave in the waters of the river: on learning whose fate he retreated. Having paid this extreme penalty for his insolence towards the Roman power, Chosroes retires with the survivors to the eastern parts, in which quarter the terms of the truce had provided that no one should attack him. Nevertheless Justinian made an irruption into the Persian territory with his entire force, and passed the whole winter there, without any molestation. He withdrew about the summer solstice, without having sustained any loss whatever, and passed the summer near the border, surrounded by prosperity and glory.

CHAPTER XV

DEATH OF CHOSROES. SUCCESSION OF HORMISDAS.

Chosroes, lost in frenzy and despair, and submerged in the surgings of sorrow, is brought to a miserable end by overwhelming anguish, after leaving behind him a lasting monument of his flight, in the law which he enacted, that no king of the Persians should henceforward lead an army against the Romans. He is succeeded by his son Hormisdas. These matters I must now pass over, since the events which follow in direct succession are inviting my attention and awaiting the regular progress of my narrative.

CHAPTER XVI

SUCCESSION OF BISHOPS.

On the decease of John, named also Catelinus, Bonosus is intrusted with the helm of the Roman see, and he is succeeded by another John, and he, again, by Pelagius. In the imperial city John is succeeded by Eutychius, who had already held the see before him. Apollinaris is succeeded in the see of Alexandria by John, and he by Eulogius. After Macarius, John is elevated to the bishopric of Jerusalem, who had pursued the monastic discipline in what is called the monastery of the Acoemets. This period passed without any changes being attempted in the state of the Church.

CHAPTER XVII

EARTHQUAKE AT ANTIOCH.

In the third year of the administration of the empire by Tiberius, a violent earthquake befell Theopolis and its suburb of Daphne, precisely at noon; on which occasion the whole of that suburb was laid in utter ruin by the shocks, while the public and private buildings in Theopolis, AD 580 though rent to the ground, were still not entirely leveled. Several other events occurred both in Theopolis, and also in the imperial city, deserving especial notice, which threw both places into confusion, and broke out into excessive disturbances: events which took their rise from zeal for God, and terminated in a manner worthy of divine agency. These I now proceed to notice.

CHAPTER XVIII

COMMOTION ON ACCOUNT OF ANATOLIUS.

There was residing at Theopolis a certain Anatolius, who was originally one of the vulgar and an artisan, but had subsequently, by some means or other, obtained admission into public offices and other posts of importance. In this city he was pursuing his engagements, from which resulted an intimacy with Gregory, president of that Church, and frequent visits to him, partly for the purpose of conversing on matters of business, and partly with a view to obtain greater influence on the ground of his intercourse with the prelate. This person was detected in the practice of sacrificial rites, and being called to account was proved to be a miscreant and a sorcerer, and implicated in innumerable enormities. He gains over, however, by bribery, the governor of the East, and would have obtained an acquittal, together with his accomplices, for he was associated with others of a similar stamp who were involved in the detection, had not the people risen, and, by exciting a universal stir, frustrated the design.

They also clamored against the bishop, saying that he was a party to the scheme; and some turbulent and malignant demon induced persons to believe that he had also taken part with Anatolius in the sacrificial rites. By this means Gregory was brought into extreme danger, from the vehement efforts of the populace against him; and the suspicion was so far prevalent, that even the emperor Tiberius was desirous of learning the truth from the mouth of Anatolius. Accordingly, he orders Anatolius and his associates to be conveyed forthwith to the imperial city. On learning this, Anatolius rushed to a certain image of the Mother of God, which was suspended by a cord in the prison, and folding his hands behind his back, announced himself as a suppliant: but she, in detestation and conviction of the guilty and God-hated man, turned herself quite round, presenting a prodigy awful and worthy of perpetual remembrance; which, having been witnessed by all the prisoners as well as by those who had the charge of Anatolius and his associates, was thus published to the world. She also appeared in a vision to some of the faithful, exhorting them against the wretch, and saying that Anatolius was guilty of insult against her Son.

When he had been conveyed to the imperial city, and, on being subjected to the extreme of torture, was unable to allege anything against the bishop, he and his associates were the cause of still greater disturbances and a general rising of the populace: for, when some of the party had received sentence of banishment instead of death, the populace, inflamed with a sort of divine zeal, caused a general commotion, in their fury and indignation, and having seized the persons condemned to banishment and put them into a skiff, they committed them alive to the flames; such being the people's verdict. They also clamored against the emperor and their own bishop Eutychius as betrayers of the faith; and they would have inevitably dispatched Eutychius, and those who had been charged with the investigation, making search for them in every quarter, had not all-preserving Providence rescued them from their pursuers, and gradually lulled the anger of so numerous a population; so that no outrage was perpetrated at their hands.

Anatolius himself, after being first exposed to the wild beasts in the amphitheater and mangled by them, was then impaled, without terminating even then his punishment in this world; for the wolves tearing down his polluted body, divided it as a feast among themselves; a circumstance never before noticed. There was also one of my fellow citizens, who, before these events took place, affirmed that he had been informed by a dream that the judgment upon Anatolius and his associates was in the hands of the populace. A person too of high distinction, being the curator of the palace, who had resolutely protected Anatolius said that he had seen the Mother of God, demanding of him how long he intended to defend Anatolius, who had so grievously outraged herself and her Son. Such was the termination of this business.

CHAPTER XIX

CHARACTER AND ACHIEVEMENTS OF MAURICE.

Tiberius being by this time in possession of the crown on the death of Justin, supersedes Justinian, since he had not been equally successful against the barbarians, and appoints Maurice to the command of the forces of the East; a person who derived his descent and name from the elder Rome, but, as regards his more immediate origin, was a native of Arabissus in Cappadocia; a man of sense and ability, and of unvarying accuracy and firmness. Being staid and precise in his mode of living and manners, he was temperate in his food, using only such as was necessary and simple, and was superior to all other indulgences of a luxurious life. He was not easily accessible to the solicitations of the vulgar, nor a too easy listener in general; well knowing that the one tends to produce contempt, and the other leads to flattery. Accordingly, he granted audiences sparingly, and those only to persons on serious business, and closed his ears against idle talk, not with wax, as poets say, but rather with reason; so that this latter was an excellent key to them, appropriately both opening and closing them during conversation. So completely had he banished both ignorance, the mother of audacity, and also cowardice, which is at the same time a foreigner and a neighbor to the former, that with him to face danger was an act of prudence, and to decline it was a measure of safety; while both courage and discretion were the charioteers of opportunity, and guided the reins to whatever quarter necessity directed: so that his efforts were both restrained and put forth, as it were, by measure and rule.

Concerning this person I shall speak more fully in the sequel; since the detail of his greatness and excellence I must reserve for the history of his reign; which displayed the man in a clearer light, as unfolding, through freedom of action, even the more inward parts of his character.

This Maurice, advancing beyond the limits of the empire, captures both cities and fortresses, of the greatest importance to the Persians, and carried off so much plunder, that the captives were sufficiently numerous to occupy at length whole islands, towns, and districts which had been deserted: and thus the land which had been previously untilled, was every where restored to cultivation. Numerous armies also were raised from among them, that fought resolutely and courageously against the other nations. At the same time every household was completely furnished with domestics, on account of the easy rate at which slaves were procured.

CHAPTER XX

OVERTHROW OF THE PERSIANS.

He also engaged Tamchosroes and Adaarmanes, the principal Persian commanders, who had advanced against him with a considerable force: but the nature, manner, and place of these transactions I leave others to record, or shall perhaps myself make them the subject of a distinct work, since my present one professes to treat of matters of a very different kind. Tamchosroes, however, falls in battle, not by the bravery of the Roman soldiery, but merely through the piety and faith of their commander: and Adaarmanes, being worsted in the fight and having lost many of his men, flies with precipitation, and this too, although Alamundarus, the commander of the Scenite barbarians, played the traitor in declining to cross the Euphrates and support Maurice against the Scenites of the opposite party. For this people are invincible by any other than themselves, on account of the fleetness of their horses: when hemmed in, they cannot be captured; and they outstrip their enemies in retreat. Theodoric too, commander of the Scythian troops, did not so much as venture within range of the missiles, but fled with all his people.

CHAPTER XXI

PRODIGIES FORESHOWING THE ELEVATION OF MAURICE TO THE EMPIRE.

Prodigies also occurred, which indicated that the imperial power was destined to Maurice. As he was offering incense, at the dead of night, within the sanctuary of Mary, the holy and immaculate virgin and Mother of God, which is called by the Antiochenes the church of Justinian, the veil which surrounds the holy table became wrapped in flames; so that Maurice was seized with amazement and awe, and was terrified at the sight. Gregory, the archbishop of the city, who was standing by, said that it was a divine manifestation, betokening to him the highest, fortune.

Christ our God also appeared to him, when in the East, calling upon him to avenge Him: which circumstance distinctly intimated the possession of sovereign power; for of what other person would He have made the demand than of an emperor, and one who manifested so much piety towards Him?

His parents also detailed to me circumstances remarkable and worthy of being recorded, when I was making inquiries on this point: for his father said that about the time of his conception, he had seen in a dream a very large vine growing from his bed, on which hung great numbers of beautiful clusters of grapes: and his mother told me that, at the time of her delivery, the earth sent forth a strange odor of peculiar sweetness; and that Empusa, as she is called, had often carried off the child for the purpose of devouring him, but had been unable to injure him.[2]

Simeon, too, who practiced the station upon the pillar in the neighborhood of Theopolis, a most energetic man, and distinguished by every divine virtue, both said and did many things which betokened his succession to the empire. The sequel of the history will relate respecting him whatever circumstances are suitable.

CHAPTER XXII

ACCESSION OF MAURICE.

Maurice assumes the sovereignty, when Tiberius was at the point of death, and had bestowed upon him his daughter Augusta, and the empire as her dowry. Notwithstanding the shortness of his reign, Tiberius left behind him an immortal memorial in the remembrance of his _{AD 582} good deeds; for he bequeathed to the commonwealth, in the appointment of Maurice, an inheritance not admitting of specification in terms, but most precious. He also distributed his own appellations, giving to Maurice the name of Tiberius, and to Augusta that of Constantina. The transactions of their reign the sequel of the history will set forth, with the aid of the divine impulse.

CHAPTER XXIII

CHRONOLOGICAL STATEMENT.

In order also to an accurate account of the various periods of time, be it known that Justin the younger, reigned alone twelve years, ten months and a half, and in conjunction with Tiberius, three years and eleven months: so that the whole period is sixteen years, nine months and a half. Tiberius also reigned four years alone: so that the whole time from Romulus to the proclamation of Maurice Tiberius, amounts to * * * years;[3] as appears from the previous and present dates.

CHAPTER XXIV
SUCCESSION OF WRITERS ON SACRED
AND PROFANE HISTORY.

By the aid of God, an account of the affairs of the Church, presenting a fair survey of the whole, has been preserved for us in what has been recorded by Eusebius Pamphili down to the time of Constantine, and thence forward as far as Theodosius the younger, by Theodoret, Sozomen, and Socrates, and in the matters which have been selected for my present work.

Primitive and profane history has been also preserved in a continuous narrative by those who have been zealous at the task; Moses being the first to compose history, as has been clearly shown by those who have collected whatever bears upon the subject, in writing a true account of events from the beginning of the world, derived from what he learned in converse with God on Mount Sinai. Then follow the accounts which those who after him prepared the way for our religion have stored up in sacred scriptures. Josephus also composed an extensive history, in every way valuable. All the stories, whether fabulous or true, relating to the contests of the Greeks and ancient barbarians, both among themselves and against each other, and whatever else had been achieved since the period at which they record the first existence of mankind, have been written by Charax, Theopompus, Ephorus, and others too numerous to mention.

The transactions of the Romans, embracing the history of the whole world and whatever else took place either with respect to their intestine divisions or their proceedings towards other nations, have been treated of by Dionysius of Halicarnassus, who has brought down his account from the times of what are called the Aborigines, to those of Pyrrhus of Epirus. The history is then taken up by Polybius of Megalopolis, who brings it down to the capture of Carthage.

All these materials Appian has portioned out by a clear arrangement, separately grouping each series of transactions, though occurring at intervals of time. What events occurred subsequent to the before-mentioned periods, have been treated by Diodorus Siculus, as far as the time of Julius Cæsar, and by Dion Cassius, who continued his account as far as Antoninus of Emesa. In a similar work of Herodian, the account, extends as far as the death of Maximus ; and in that of Nicostratus, the sophist of Trapezus, from Philip, the successor of Gordian, to Odenatus of Palmyra, and the ignominious expedition of Valerian against the Persians. Dexippus has also written at great length on the same subject, commencing with the Scythian wars, and terminating with the reign of Claudius, the successor of Gallienus: and he also included the military transactions of the Carpi and other barbarian tribes, in Greece, Thrace, and Ionia. Eusebius too, commencing from Octavian, Trajan, and Marcus, brought his account down to the death of Carus. The history of the same times has been partially written both by Arrian and Asinius Quadratus: that of the succeeding period by Zosimus, as far as Honorius and Arcadius: and events subsequent to their reign by Priscus the Rhetorician, and others.

The whole of this range of history has been excellently epitomized by Eustathius of Epiphania, in two volumes, one extending to the capture of Troy, the other to the twelfth year of the reign of Anastasius, The occurrences subsequent to that period have been written by Procopius the rhetorician as far as the time of Justinian; and the account has been thenceforward continued by Agathias the rhetorician, and John, my fellow-citizen and kinsman, as far as the flight of Chosroes the younger to the Romans, and his restoration to his kingdom: on which occasion Maurice was by no means tardy in his operations, but royally entertained the fugitive, and with the utmost speed restored him to his kingdom, at great cost and with numerous forces. These writers, however, have not yet published their history. With respect to these events, I also will detail in the sequel, such matters as are suitable, with the favor of the higher power.

NOTES

1. A verb is missing here in Walford's original text. I have inserted "enjoy" to maintain the sense of the sentence. Whitby translates this passage somewhat differently. See Whitby, p. 264.
2. In Greek mythology, Empusa, a familiar of the witch-goddess Hecate, was a ghoulish shape-shifting creature which lured people to their deaths by assuming a pleasing form (March, p. 285).
3. There is a lacuna here. According to Whitby's translation, the number of years indicated should be 1,143 (Whitby, p. 285, fn 82).

THE SIXTH BOOK

CHAPTER I

NUPTIALS OF MAURICE AND AUGUSTA.

Maurice, on succeeding to the empire, in the first place made the necessary arrangements for his nuptials, and, in accordance with the imperial ordinance, marries Augusta, named also Constantina, with magnificent ceremony, and with public banquetings and festivity in every part of the city. In attendance on the nuptials were Religion and Royalty, offering an escort most distinguished and gifts most precious. For the one supplied a father and mother, to hallow the rite with honored locks of grey and venerable wrinkles—circumstance strange in the story of sovereigns—also brethren noble and blooming, to give dignity to the nuptial procession: the other, a gold embroidered robe, adorned with purple and Indian gems, and crowns most costly, with abundance of gold and the varied emblazonment of jewels; together with the attendance of all who were distinguished in courtly rank or military service, lighting the nuptial flambeaux in splendid costumes and investitures, and hymning the bridal cavalcade: so that no human display was ever more majestic and happy.

Damophilus, when writing on the subject of Rome, says

that Plutarch the Chæronean[1] has well remarked, that in order to her greatness alone did Virtue and Fortune unite in friendly truce: but, for myself, I would say that in respect of Maurice alone did Piety and Good Fortune so conspire; by Piety laying compulsion upon Fortune, and not permitting her to shift at all. It was henceforward the settled aim of the emperor to wear the purple and the diadem not merely on his person but also on his soul: for he alone of recent sovereigns was sovereign of himself; and, with authority most truly centered in himself, he banished from his own soul the mob-rule of the passions, and having established an aristocracy in his own reasonings, he showed himself a living image of virtue, training his subjects to imitation.

Nor have I said this by way of flattery: for how could such be my motive, since he is not acquainted with what is being written? That such was, however, the case with Maurice, will be evidenced by the gifts bestowed upon him by God, and the circumstances of various kinds that must unquestionably be referred to divine favor.[2]

CHAPTER II

ALAMUNDARUS THE ARAB AND HIS SON NAAMANES.

Besides his other noble purposes, this was an especial object with the emperor, to avoid in every case the shedding of the blood of persons guilty of treason. Accordingly, he did not put to death Alamundarus, chieftain of the Scenite Arabs, who had betrayed both the commonwealth and Maurice himself, as I have already detailed; but sentenced him to deportation to an island with his wife and some of his children, and appointed Sicily as the place of his banishment.

Naamanes his son, notwithstanding a unanimous sentence of death, he detained as a prisoner at large, without any further infliction; although he had filled the empire with endless mischiefs, and, by the hands of his followers, had plundered either Phœnicia and Palestine, and enslaved the inhabitants, at the time when Alamundarus was captured. He pursued the same course in innumerable other cases, which shall be severally noticed in their places.

CHAPTER III

MILITARY OPERATIONS OF JOHN AND PHILIPPICUS.

Maurice sent out as commander of the forces of the East, first, John, a Scythian, who, after experiencing some reverses, with some alternations of success, achieved nothing worthy of mention; afterwards, Philippicus, who was allied to him by having married one of his two sisters. Having crossed the border and laid waste all before him, he amassed great booty, and killed many of the nobles of Nisibis and the other cities situated within the Tigris. He also gave battle to the Persians, and, after a severe conflict, attended with AD 585 the loss of many distinguished men on the side of the enemy, he made numerous prisoners, and dismissed unharmed a battalion, which had retreated to an eminence and was fairly in his power, under a promise that they would urge their sovereign to send immediate proposals for peace.

He also completed other measures during the continuance of his command, namely, in withdrawing his troops from superfluities and things tending to luxury, and in reducing them to discipline and subordination: the representation of which transactions must be fixed by writers, past or present, according as they may be or have been circumstanced with respect to hearsay or opinion—writers whose narrative, stumbling and limping through ignorance, or rendered affected by partiality, or blinded by antipathy, misses the mark of truth.

CHAPTER IV

MUTINY OF THE TROOPS AGAINST PRISCUS.

He is succeeded in the command by Priscus, a person difficult of access, and not readily approached without necessary occasion, who expected the successful accomplishment of all his measures if he should maintain an almost entire seclusion; from a notion, that through the awe thence resulting, the soldiery also would be more obedient to orders. Accordingly, on his arrival at the camp with stern and haughty look and in imposing costume, he issued certain orders, relating to the hardihood of the soldiery in the field, to strictness in respect of their arms and to their allowances. Having received previous intimation of the proceeding, they then gave unrestrained vent to their rage; and advancing in a body to the general's quarters, they pillage, in barbarian fashion, all his magnificence and the most valuable of his treasures, and would inevitably have dispatched Priscus himself, had he not mounted one of the led horses, and escaped to Edessa: to which place they laid siege, demanding his surrender.

AD 587

CHAPTER V

COMPULSORY ELEVATION OF GERMANUS.

On the refusal of their demands by the citizens, they leave Priscus there, and seizing Germanus, who at that time held the command in Phœnicia Libanensis, they elect him their own general and emperor, while he resisted and they were the more urgent; and a struggle thus arose, on the part of the one to escape compulsion, of the others to enforce their object. After they had menaced him with death unless he would embrace the offered charge, and he, on his part, eagerly embraced the alternative, disclaiming all fear and consternation, they proceeded to certain severities and methods of cruelty, which they thought he would not be able to bear; for they did not suppose that he would manifest greater endurance than the strength of nature and his time of life would warrant. By putting him to the trial at first cautiously and sparingly, they succeed in forcing him to accede to their demands, and solemnly to swear that he would be true to them. Thus they compelled him to be their ruler under rule, their subject sovereign, their master in thraldom. Then chasing from them the officers of every grade, they elect others in their place, openly reviling the imperial government. They treated provincials on the whole less harshly than the barbarians did, but in a manner very unlike allies or servants of the commonwealth: for they levied their provisions not according to stated measures or weight, and were not contented with the quarters assigned to them: but the will of each individual was a rule, and his caprice an established measure.

CHAPTER VI

MISSION OF PHILIPPICUS.

The emperor dispatches Philippicus to settle this ferment: they, however, not only denied him reception, but periled the lives of all whom they supposed to be connected with him.

CHAPTER VII

ACCUSATIONS AGAINST GREGORY, PATRIARCH OF ANTIOCH.

While matters were in this situation, Gregory, bishop of Theopolis, returns from the imperial city, after having been victorious in the struggle which I now proceed to detail.

At the time when Asterius held the government of the East, a quarrel had arisen between him and Gregory: the higher ranks of the city sided entirely with the former, and were supported by the populace, and by those who were engaged in trades; for each class declared that they had been injured by Gregory; until at last license was given to the rabble to vent their abuse against him. Thus both the other classes accorded with the populace, and they clamored forth their insults against the prelate in the streets and the theater; and even the actors indulged in them. Asterius is removed from his government, and John is invested with it, with orders from the emperor to make inquiry into the stir; a man incompetent to the management of the most trifling matters, much less a business so important. Having, in consequence, filled the city with confusion and uproar, and given public license to any one that chose, to accuse the bishop, he receives a formal charge against him from a certain banker, to the effect that he had had criminal intercourse with his own sister, married to another man. He also receives accusations from other persons of the same stamp against Gregory, as having repeatedly disturbed the peace of the city. On the latter charge he declared his readiness to make his defense: with respect to the others, he appealed to the emperor and a synod.

Accordingly, he repaired to the imperial city, to make answer to these charges, accompanied by myself as his adviser, and is victorious after a prolonged struggle during an investigation of the matter before the patriarchs from every quarter, who appeared either in person or by deputy, as well as the sacred senate, and many most religious metropolitans: and the result was that the accuser, after having been scourged and paraded round the city, was sent into exile. Gregory thence returns to his see, at the time when the troops were in a state of mutiny, and Philippicus was remaining in the neighborhood of Berœa and Chalcis.

CHAPTER VIII

RECURRENCE OF EARTHQUAKES AT ANTIOCH.

At an interval of four months from the return of Gregory, in the six hundred and thirty-seventh year of the era of Theopolis, sixty-one years after the former earthquake, a crash and concussion shook the entire city, about the third hour of the night, on the last day of the month Hyperberetæus, at the time when I was celebrating my marriage with a AD 589 young maiden, and the whole city was making rejoicings and holding a festival at the public cost, in honor of the nuptial ceremony. This convulsion leveled by far the greater part of the buildings, their very foundations being cast up by it, and all the portions of the most holy church were thrown to the ground, with the exception of the hemisphere, which, after its injury by the earthquake in the time of Justin, had been secured by Ephraemius with timbers from Daphne. By the subsequent shocks, it received an inclination in a northerly direction; so that the timbers were thrown by it into a leaning position, and fell, when the hemisphere had returned, by the force of the shock, exactly into its original situation, as if it had been adjusted by a rule.

Nearly the entire quarter named Ostracine was ruined, and Psephium, of which I have made previous mention, as well as all the parts called Brysia, and the buildings of the venerable sanctuary of the Mother of God, with the sole exception of the central colonnade, which was singularly preserved. All the towers of the plain were also damaged, though the other buildings in that quarter escaped, with the exception of the battlements, of which some stones were thrown backwards, though they did not fall. Other churches also suffered injury, and one of the public baths, namely, that which had separate divisions according to the seasons.

An incalculable number of persons were involved in the destruction, and according to an estimate which some persons drew from the supply of bread, about sixty thousand perished. The bishop experienced a most unexpected preservation in the midst of the fall of the entire habitation where he then was, and the destruction of every individual except those who were near his person. These took up the bishop in their arms, and lowered him by a cord, after a second shock had rent an opening, and thus they removed him beyond the reach of danger.

Another preservation was also granted to the city, our compassionate God having mitigated the keenness of His threatened vengeance, and corrected our sin with the branch of pity and mercy: for no conflagration followed, though so many fires were spread about the place, in hearths, public and private lamps, kitchens, furnaces, baths, and innumerable other forms. Very many persons of distinction, and among them Asterius himself, became the victims of the calamity. The emperor endeavored to alleviate this visitation by grants of money.

CHAPTER IX

INROAD AND DESTRUCTION OF THE BARBARIANS.

In the army, matters continued in the same state; and, in consequence, the barbarians made an inroad, in the expectation that there would be no one to check them in the exercise of barbarian practices. Germanus, however, encounters them with his forces, and inflicted a defeat so destructive, that not a man was left to convey to the Persians tidings of the misfortune.

CHAPTER X

CLEMENCY OF THE EMPEROR TOWARDS THE REBELS. INVASION OF THE AVARS.

Accordingly, the emperor remunerates the troops with largesses of money; and, withdrawing Germanus and others, brings them to trial. They were all condemned to death: but the emperor would not permit any infliction whatever; on the contrary, he bestowed rewards on them.

During the course of these transactions, the Avars twice made an inroad as far as the Long Wall, and captured Anchialus, Singidunum, and many towns and fortresses throughout the whole of Greece, enslaving the inhabitants, and laying every thing waste with fire and sword; in consequence of the greater part of the forces being AD 590 engaged in the East. Accordingly, the emperor sends Andrew, the first of the imperial guards, on an attempt to induce the troops to receive their former officers.

CHAPTER XI

MISSION OF THE PATRIARCH GREGORY TO THE TROOPS.

Since, however, the troops would not endure the bare mention of the proposal, the business is transferred to Gregory, not only as being a person competent to the execution of the most important measures, but because he had earned the highest regard from the soldiery; since some of them had received presents from him in money, others in clothing, provisions, and other things, when they were passing his neighborhood at the time of their enlistment. Accordingly, he assembles, by summons dispatched to every quarter, the principal persons of the army at Litarba, a place distant from Theopolis about three hundred stadia; and though confined to his couch, addressed them in person, in the following words.

CHAPTER XII

ORATION OF GREGORY TO THE TROOPS.

"I have been expecting, O Romans—Romans both in name and deeds—that your visit to me would have been made long ago, for the purpose of communicating to me your present circumstances, and of receiving that friendly counsel of which you have an assurance in my kindliness towards you, so unequivocally evinced by past occurrences, at the time when I relieved, by a supply of necessaries, your tempest-struck and wave-tossed plight. Since, however, this course has not hitherto been taken—it may be that Providence has not permitted it, in order that the Persians, having been utterly defeated by men without a leader, might be thereby thoroughly taught the prowess of the Romans, and that your pure loyalty might be completely proved, in having been tested by the juncture and testified by your deeds; for you showed that, notwithstanding your quarrel with your officers, you do not regard any thing as more important than the good of the commonwealth—let us accordingly now deliberate what ought to be your conduct.

"Your sovereign invites you with a promise of an amnesty of all past transactions, receiving the display of your loyalty to the commonwealth and your prowess in the field as emblems of supplication. While bestowing upon you these most certain pledges of pardon the emperor thus speaks: 'Since God has given victory to their loyalty, and, on the abandonment of their errors, a signal display has been granted to their prowess as a clear intimation of forgiveness, how can I do otherwise than follow the judgment of heaven? A king's heart is in the hand of God, and He sways it whithersoever He will.'

"Yield, therefore, to me at once, O Romans. Let us not willfully forfeit the present opportunity, nor allow it to elude our grasp: for opportunity, when it has once slipped from us, is most unwilling to be seized, and, as if it were indignant at having been neglected, is ever after intolerant of capture. Show yourselves the heirs of the obedience of your fathers, as ye are of their courage; in order that ye may appear altogether Romans, and no taunt may touch you or point at you as degenerate. Your fathers, under the command of consuls and emperors, by obedience and courage became masters of the whole world. Manlius Torquatus, though he crowned, yet also put to death his son, who had played a valiant part but in disobedience of orders. For by skill on the part of the leaders, combined with obedience in those whom they lead, great successes are ordinarily achieved; but either, when bereaved of the other, is lame and unsteady, and is utterly overthrown by the separation of the excellent pair.

"Be not, therefore, tardy, but at once obey my call, while the priestly office mediates between the emperor and the army; and show that your proceedings were not the establishment of a rival sovereign, but a transient display of just indignation against commanders who had wronged you: for unless you immediately embrace the offer, I shall at once consider myself as quit of the service laid upon me in this matter by my duty to the commonwealth and my regard for you. Consider too yourselves, what has been the fate of pretenders to the sovereignty. What too will be the termination of your present position? To continue concentrated is impossible: for whence will you derive your provision of ordinary fruits, or those supplies which the sea furnishes to the land, except by war between Christians, and the mutual infliction of the most disgraceful treatment? What too will be the final result? You will live in dispersion, and haunted by Justice, who will henceforward disdain to bestow forgiveness. Let us therefore give pledges of amity, and consider what course will be for the benefit of ourselves and the state, at a time too when we shall have the days of the saving Passion and of the most holy Resurrection conspiring with the deed."

CHAPTER XIII

SUBMISSION OF THE TROOPS.

Having thus addressed them, accompanying his speech with many tears, he wrought, an instantaneous change in the minds of all, as it had been by some divine impulse. They immediately requested permission to retire from the meeting, and to deliberate among themselves respecting the course to be pursued. After a short interval they returned, and placed themselves at the disposal of the bishop. However, on his naming Philippicus to them, in order that they might themselves request him for a commander, they declared that the whole army had on this point bound themselves with fearful oaths: but the bishop, undeterred by this, without the least delay said that he was a bishop by divine permission, and had authority to loose and bind both upon earth and in heaven, and at the same time he quoted the sacred oracle. On their yielding upon this point also, he propitiated the Deity with supplication and prayers, at the same time administering to them the communion of the immaculate body; for it happened to be the second day of the holy passion week. After he had feasted them all, to the number of two thousand, upon couches hastily constructed on the turf, he returned home the following day.

It was also agreed that the soldiers should assemble wherever they might choose. Gregory in consequence sends for Philippicus, who at that time was at Tarsus in Cilicia, intending to proceed immediately to the imperial city; and he also reports these proceedings to the government, communicating at the same time the prayer of the soldiery respecting Philippicus. Accordingly, they meet Philippicus at Theopolis, and employing those who had been admitted to partake in the divine regeneration to entreat for them, they bend in supplication before him, and, on receiving a solemn promise of amnesty, they return to their duty with him. Such was the progress of these events.

CHAPTER XIV

LOSS OF MARTYROPOLIS.

A certain Sittas, one of the petty officers stationed at Martyropolis, considering himself aggrieved by the commanders in that place, betrays the city, by watching the withdrawal of the troops which occupied it, and introducing a Persian battalion under color of being Romans. He thus obtained possession of a place which was most important to the Romans; and, retaining most of the younger females, expelled all the other inhabitants, except a few domestic slaves.

Philippicus in consequence marched thither, and beleaguered the city, without being provided with things necessary for the siege. Nevertheless, he maintained his operations with such means as he possessed, AD 590 and, having run several mines, threw down one of the towers. He was unable, however, to make himself master of the place, because the Persians continued their exertions through the night, and secured the breach. When the Romans, repeatedly assaulting, were as often repulsed, for the missiles were hurled upon them from vantage ground with unerring aim, and since they were suffering greater loss than they inflicted, they at last raised the siege, and encamped at a short distance, with the sole object of preventing the Persians from reinforcing the garrison. By the order of Maurice, Gregory visits the camp, and induces them to resume the siege. They were, however, unable to accomplish anything, from their utter want of engines for sieges. In consequence, the army breaks up for winter quarters, and numerous garrisons are left in the neighboring forts, to prevent the Persians from secretly introducing succors into the place.

In the succeeding summer, on the re-assembling of the army, and the advance of the Persians, a severely contested battle is fought before Martyropolis. Though the advantage was on the side of Philippicus, and many Persians had fallen, with the loss of one distinguished chieftain a considerable body of the enemy made their way into the city: which was in fact their main object. Thenceforward the Romans gave up the siege in despair, as being unable to encounter this force, and they erect a rival city at the distance of seven stadia, in a stronger situation on the mountains, in order to the carrying on of counter operations. Such were the proceedings of the army during the summer; it broke up on the approach of winter.

CHAPTER XV

CAPTURE OF OCBAS.

Comentiolus, a Thracian by birth, is sent out as a successor in the command to Philippicus. He engaged the Persians with great spirit, and would have lost his life by being thrown to the ground together with his horse, had not one of the guards mounted him upon a led horse, and conveyed him out of the battle. In consequence, the enemy fly with precipitation, with the loss of all their commanders, and retire to Nisibis; and, fearing to return to their king, since he had threatened them with death unless they should bring off their commanders in safety, they there enter into the insurrection against Hormisdas, now that Varamus, the Persian general, had already entertained that design with his party on his return from his encounter with the Turks.

In the meantime, Comentiolus, having commenced the siege of Martyropolis, leaves there the greater part of his army, and himself makes an excursion with a chosen body of troops to Ocbas, a very strong fortress, situated on a precipice on the bank opposite to Martyropolis, and commanding a view of the whole of that city. Having employed every effort in the siege, and thrown down some portion of the wall by catapults, he takes the place by storming the breach. In consequence, the Persians thenceforward despaired of keeping possession of Martyropolis.

CHAPTER XVI

MURDER OF HORMISDAS.

While such was the course of these events, the Persians dispatched Hormisdas, the most unjust of all monarchs, in as far as he inflicted upon his subjects not only pecuniary exactions, but, also various modes of death.

AD 591

CHAPTER XVII

FLIGHT OF CHOSROES THE YOUNGER.

They establish as his successor his son Chosroes, against whom Varamus advanced with his troops. Chosroes encounters him with an inconsiderable force, and takes to flight on seeing his own men deserting him. He arrives at Circesium, having, according to his own account, vowed to the God of the Christians, that he would allow his horse to take its course wherever it should be guided by Him. He was accompanied by his wives and two newly-born children, and certain Persian nobles who voluntarily followed him.

Thence he sends an embassy to the emperor Maurice; who, manifesting on this occasion too the soundest judgment, and deriving from the very circumstances an estimate of the instability and mutability of life, and the sudden fluctuations of human affairs, admits his suit, and treats him as a guest instead of an exile, and as a son instead of a fugitive, welcoming him with royal gifts, which were sent not only by the emperor himself, but, in similar style, by the empress to the consorts of Chosroes, and also by their children to the children.

CHAPTER XVIII

MISSION OF GREGORY AND DOMITIAN TO MEET CHOSROES.

The emperor also dispatches the whole of his body guards and the entire Roman army with their commander with orders to attend Chosroes wherever he might choose to proceed: and by way of still greater distinction, he also sends Domitian, bishop of Melitene, his own kinsman, a man of sense and ability, most capable both in word and deed, and most efficient for the dispatch of the highest transactions. He sends Gregory too: who on all points filled Chosroes with amazement, by his conversation, by his munificence, and by his suggestion of seasonable measures.

CHAPTER XIX

RESTORATION OF CHOSROES.

Chosroes, having proceeded as far as Hierapolis, the capital of Euphratensis, immediately returned: and this was done with the consent of Maurice, who favored the interest of his suppliant more than his own glory. He also presents Chosroes with a large sum of money, a circumstance never before recorded; and having raised a body of Persians, and supplied the cost from his own means, he sends him across the border with a combined force of Romans and Persians, after Martyropolis had been previously surrendered, together with the traitor Sittas; whom the inhabitants stoned and impaled.

AD 591

Daras was also recovered on its evacuation by the Persian garrison, and Chosroes was restored to his kingdom in consequence of the utter overthrow of Varamus, in a single engagement with the Roman troops only, and his inglorious and solitary flight.

CHAPTER XX

GOLANDUCH THE MARTYR.

At that time there was living in our country Golanduch, a female martyr, who maintained her testimony through a course of severe sufferings when tortured by the Persian Magi, and was a worker of extraordinary miracles. Her life was written by Stephen, the former bishop of Hierapolis.[3]

CHAPTER XXI

OFFERINGS OF CHOSROES.

Chosroes, on his restoration to his kingdom, sends to Gregory a cross, embellished with much gold and precious stones, in honor of the victorious martyr Sergius; which cross Theodora, the wife of Justinian, had dedicated and Chosroes had carried off with the other treasures, as I have already related. He also sends another golden cross, on which was engraven the following inscription in Greek:

"This cross I, Chosroes, king of kings, son of Hormisdas, have sent. After I had been compelled to take refuge in the Roman territory by the slanderous practices and villainy of the unhappy Varamus and his cavalry, and when, because the unhappy Zadespram had come to Nisibis with an army, with a view to seduce the cavalry in that quarter to revolt and raise commotion, we also had sent a body of cavalry with a commander to Charchas; at that time, by the fortune of the venerable and renowned saint, Sergius, having heard that he granted the petitions addressed to him, we vowed, in the first year of our reign, on the seventh day of January, that if our cavalry should slay or capture Zadespram, we would send to his sanctuary a golden cross, embellished with jewels for the sake of his venerable name: and on the seventh day of February they brought to us the head of Zadespram.

Having, accordingly, obtained our petition, in order that each circumstance should be placed beyond all doubt, we have sent, in honor of his venerable name, this cross, which we have caused to be made, and together with it that which was sent to his sanctuary by Justinian, emperor of the Romans, and which was conveyed hither by our father Chosroes, king of kings, son of Cabades, at the time of the rupture between the two states, and has been found among our treasures."

Gregory, having received these crosses, with the approval

of the emperor Maurice, dedicated them with much ceremony in the sanctuary of the martyr. Shortly after, Chosroes sent, other offerings for the same temple, with a golden disc, bearing the following inscription:

"I, Chosroes, king of kings, son of Hormisdas, have placed the inscription upon this disc, not as an object for the gaze of mankind, nor that the greatness of thy venerable name might be made known by words of mine, but on account of the truth of the matters therein recorded, and the many benefits and favors which I have received at thy hands: for that my name should be inscribed on thy sacred vessels is a happiness to me. At the time when I was at Beramais, I begged of thee, O holy one, that thou wouldest come to my aid, and that Sira might conceive: and inasmuch as Sira was a Christian and I a heathen, and our law forbids us to have a Christian wife, nevertheless, on account of my favorable feelings towards thee, I disregarded the law as respects her, and among my wives I have constantly esteemed, and do still esteem her as peculiarly mine.

"Thus I resolved to request of thy goodness, O Saint, that she might conceive: and I made the request with a vow that if Sira should conceive, I would send the cross she wears to thy venerable sanctuary. On this account both I and Sira purposed to retain this cross in memory of thy name, O Saint, and in place of it to send five thousand staters, as its value, which does not really exceed four thousand four hundred staters. From the time that I conceived this request and these intentions, until I reached Rhosochosron, not more than ten days elapsed, when thou, O Saint, not on account of my worthiness but thy kindness, appearedst to me in a vision of the night and didst thrice tell me that Sira should conceive, while in the same vision thrice I replied, 'It is well.' From that day forward Sira has not experienced the custom of women, because thou art the granter of requests; though I, had I not believed thy words, and that thou art holy and the granter of requests, should have doubted that she would not thenceforward experience the custom of women.

"From this circumstance I was convinced of the power of the vision and the truth of thy words, and accordingly forthwith sent the same cross and its value to thy venerable sanctuary, with directions that out of that sum should be made a disc, and a cup for the purposes of the divine mysteries, as also a cross to be fixed upon the holy table, and a censer, all of gold: also a Hunnish veil adorned with gold. Let the surplus of the sum belong to thy sanctuary, in order that by virtue of thy fortune, O Saint, thou mayest come to the aid of me and Sira in all matters and especially with respect to this petition; and that what has been already procured for us by thy intercession, may be consummated according to the compassion of thy goodness, and the desire of me and Sira; so that both of us, and all persons in the world, may trust in thy power and continue to believe in thee."

Such is the language of the offerings sent by Chosroes: an instance altogether resembling the prophecy of Balaam; since our compassionate God has wisely disposed it, that the tongues of heathens should give utterance to saving words.[4]

CHAPTER XXII

NAAMANES THE ARAB.

At the same time Naamanes, chieftain of the Scenites, after having been a detestable and vile heathen, to such an extent as to sacrifice with his own hand human beings to his gods, approached the sacred baptism. At which time he melted down a Venus of solid gold, and divided it among the poor, and also brought over all his followers to the service of God.

Gregory too, after the presentation of the crosses of Chosroes, while making, with the approbation of the government, a visitation of the solitudes on the borders, where the doctrines of Severus extensively prevailed, brought

223

into union with the Church of God many garrisons, villages, monasteries, and entire tribes.

CHAPTER XXIII

SIMEON THE STYLITE THE YOUNGER.

At this time, when the sainted Simeon was afflicted with a mortal disease, Gregory, on being informed by me of the circumstance, hastens to salute him for the last time, but was nevertheless disappointed. This Simeon far surpassed all his contemporaries in virtue, and endured the discipline of a life on the top of a column from his earliest years, since he even cast his teeth in that situation.

The occasion on which he was first elevated on the column was the following. While still very young, he was roving about, sporting and bounding along the eminences of the mountain, and meeting with a panther, he throws his girdle round its neck, and with this kind of halter led the beast, beguiled of its ferocity, to his monastery. His preceptor, who himself occupied a column, observing the circumstance, enquired what he had got; to which he replied, that it was a cat. Conjecturing from this occurrence how distinguished the child would be for virtue, he took him up upon the column; and on this column, and on another, towering above the summit of the mountain, he spent sixty-eight years; earning thereby the highest gifts of grace, in respect of the ejection of demons, the healing of every disease and malady, and the foresight of future things as if they were present.

He also foretold to Gregory that the latter would not witness his death, but said that he was ignorant of the events which should follow it.

On occasion also of my ponderings on the loss of my children, when I was perplexed with the suggestion, why such things did not befall heathens who had numerous offspring; though I had not disclosed my thoughts to any one, he wrote advising me to abandon such ideas as being displeasing to God.

In the case of the wife of one of my amanuenses, when the milk would not flow after child-birth, and the child was in extreme danger, laying his hand upon the right hand of her husband, he bid him place it upon the breasts of his wife. When this was done, immediately the milk started, as if from a fountain, so as to saturate her dress.

A child having been forgotten at dead of night by its fellow-travelers, a lion took it on its back, and conveyed it to the monastery; when, by orders of Simeon, the servants went out and brought in the child under the protection of the lion.

Many other actions he performed, surpassing everything that has been recorded; which demand of an historian elegance of language, leisure, and a separate treatise, being renowned by the tongues of mankind; for persons came to visit him from almost every part of the earth, not only Romans but barbarians, and obtained the object of their prayers. In his case, the place of food and drink was supplied by the branches of a shrub which grew upon the mountain.

CHAPTER XXIV

DEATH OF THE PATRIARCH GREGORY.

Shortly after, Gregory also dies, after taking a draught of medicine composed of what is called Hermodactylus, administered by one of the physicians during a fit of gout; a disease with which he was much afflicted.[5] At AD 594 the time of his death, Gregory, the successor of Pelagius, was bishop of Old Rome, and John of New Rome; Eulogius, one of those whom I have already mentioned, of Alexandria; and Anastasius was restored, after three and twenty years, to the see of Theopolis. John was bishop of Jerusalem; since whose decease, which occurred shortly after, no one has hitherto been entrusted with that see.

Here let me close my history, in the twelfth year of the reign of Maurice Tiberius, leaving the task of selecting and recording succeeding events to those who choose to undertake it. If any matter has been overlooked by me or has been treated without sufficient accuracy, let no one blame me, considering that I have brought together scattered materials in order to the benefit of mankind; for whose sake I have submitted to so much toil.

I have also compiled another volume, containing memorials, epistles, decrees, orations, and disputations, and some other matters. The memorials were principally composed in the name of Gregory, bishop of Theopolis; and by means of them I obtained two dignities, Tiberius Constantine having conferred upon me quæstorian rank, and Maurice Tiberius that of prefecture, in consideration of what I composed at the time when he rid the empire of reproach in becoming the father of Theodosius, an earnest of all prosperity both to himself and the commonwealth.

NOTES

1. De Fortuna Romanorum, sub init.
2. A much more detailed history of the reign of the emperor Maurice and his overthrow at the hands of the tyrant Phocas may be found in *The History of Theophylact Simocatta* as translated into English by Michael and Mary Whitby (1986).
3. See pp. 148–149 in Whitby's *The History of Theophylact Simocatta* for more details on the life of St. Golanduch, along with a discussion of the surviving versions of her biography as composed by Stephen of Hierapolis.
4. Num. 22–24.
5. Hermodactylus, meaning "finger of Hermes," was a type of plant used in antiquity to treat gout and other illnesses (Adams, p. 357).

GENERAL INDEX

Also available in the Christian Roman Empire Series

The Life of Belisarius
    by Lord Mahon (1848)

The Gothic History of Jordanes
    by Charles Christopher Mierow (1915)

The Book of the Popes (Liber Pontificalis)
    by Louise Ropes Loomis (1916)

The Chronicle of John, Bishop of Nikiu
    by R. H. Charles (1916)

For more information on this series, see our website at:
http://www.evolpub.com/CRE/CREseries.html

CPSIA information can be obtained at www.ICGtesting.com
Printed in the USA
BVOW07s0204300614

357680BV00001B/3/A

9 781889 758886